Pints & Purls

Pints & Purls

PORTABLE PROJECTS
for the
SOCIAL KNITTER

KARIDA *collins* & **LIBBY** *bruce*

Cincinnati, Ohio
www.mycraftivity.com

13 12 11 10 09   5 4 3 2 1

Distributed in Canada by Fraser Direct
100 Armstrong Avenue
Georgetown, ON, Canada L7G 5S4
Tel: (905) 877-4411

Distributed in the U.K. and Europe by David & Charles
Brunel House, Newton Abbot, Devon, TQ12 4PU, England
Tel: (+44) 1626 323200, Fax: (+44) 1626 323319
E-mail: postmaster@davidandcharles.co.uk

Distributed in Australia by Capricorn Link
P.O. Box 704, S. Windsor, NSW 2756 Australia
Tel: (02) 4577-3555

Library of Congress Cataloging-in-Publication Data
Collins, Karida.
   Pints and purls : portable projects for the social knitter / Karida Collins and Libby Bruce. – 1st ed.
      p. cm.
   Includes index.
   ISBN 978-1-60061-146-9 (pbk. : alk. paper)
   1. Knitting–Patterns. I. Bruce, Libby. II. Title.
TT825.C6476 2009
746.43'2041–dc22

2008041612

Editor: **Jessica Gordon**
Designer: **Kelly O'Dell**
Production Coordinator: **Greg Nock**
Photographer: **Ric Deliantoni**
Wardrobe Stylist: **Monica Skrzelowski**
Set Stylist: **Jan Nickum**
Make-Up Artist: **Cass Smith**
Technical Editor: **Amy Polcyn**
Cover Illustration: **Darren Welch, Dual Identity inc.**

Dedications

From Karida...
Dedicated to Rachel, who taught me to knit, introduced me to the world of craft and always says that I'm her greatest knitting accomplishment.

From Libby...
Dedicated to the memory of my grandfather, Butch Guenther. We miss you, Papa.

METRIC CONVERSION CHART

TO CONVERT	TO	MULTIPLY BY
Centimeters	Inches	0.4
Feet	Centimeters	30.5
Centimeters	Feet	0.03
Yards	Meters	0.9
Meters	Yards	1.1
Sq. Inches	Sq. Centimeters	6.45
Sq. Centimeters	Sq. Inches	0.16
Sq. Feet	Sq. Meters	0.09
Sq. Meters	Sq. Feet	10.8
Sq. Yards	Sq. Meters	0.8
Sq. Meters	Sq. Yards	1.2
Pounds	Kilograms	0.45
Kilograms	Pounds	2.2
Ounces	Grams	28.3
Grams	Ounces	0.035

an imprint of F+W Media, Inc.
www.fwmedia.com

About the Authors

Libby

Libby Bruce (below left) became ruthlessly addicted to knitting in college. Today she knits and drinks in Columbus, Ohio, where she lives with her awesome husband and two ill-behaved cats. She blogs about knitting and yarn at *winelips.blogspot.com* and teaches knitting classes through her business, Wonderknit.

In addition to knitting and drinking, Libby loves books, animals, trouble, rock 'n roll and things topped with melted cheese. One day she hopes to run the nicest alpaca farm in town.

Karida

Karida Collins (below right) is a recovering academic with a serious fiber addiction that she channels into her yarn dyeing business, Neighborhood Fiber Co., based in Washington, DC. Karida learned to knit five years ago from her best friend, and she hasn't put down the needles since. Knitting is her passion, but she loves dabbling in anything crafty, including embroidery, papercrafts, crochet and cross-stitch.

Karida lives at Neighborhood Co. headquarters with her partner Erika and a menagerie of pets. Neighborhood Fiber Co. was born because Karida thought it would be the best way to make yarn a business expense. Erika's still not sure.

Acknowledgments

From Karida...

Thanks to my partner, Erika, for being encouraging and supportive at every step. Thank you for coming up with possible book titles and buying endless domain names. Thank you for picking up the household slack while I was being an artist and for always reassuring me that I could do it. Thank you to my family and friends for smiling and nodding when I described the book concept. Especially thanks to Mom, for knitting endlessly long samples and explaining the "concept" to the rest of the family when I left the room. Thank you William for your sincere, if monosyllabic, encouragement. Karen, you rock the dishrag.

From Libby...

First and foremost, thanks to my husband, Matt, for supporting me in every possible way during the writing of this book: for living in a house full of yarn, for listening to me chatter on and on about cables and gauge, for kissing my strained wrists, for handing me glasses of wine and for lending his artistic eye to the charts. Thank you, Matty. Boundless gratitude to my family, especially Mom and Dad, for encouraging me in all my harebrained ideas and never trying to steer me toward anything practical. I'd be lost without The Goodies and Co., who always inspire me, support me and crack me up. Karen Brackbill and Jennifer Lawson are great friends and the most helpful, speedy and talented test knitters ever.

From Both of Us...

Thanks to the Knit, Purl, Hurl crowd in DC—you guys planted the seeds of this book. Thanks to all the contributing designers and our tech editor: You did a great job. Thanks to all the companies who provided yarn support, especially Cascade Yarns. Thanks to the whole crew at F+W for all the work on the book: Christine, Ginger and the whole team. Extra special thanks to our editor, Jessica Gordon, for taking a chance on a goofy idea.

REMEMBER: Please drink responsibly. Don't drink and drive.
Or knit and drive, for that matter.

Contents

10 AN INTRODUCTION TO SOCIAL KNITTING

12 WHAT IS SOCIAL KNITTING?

14 DRINK RATINGS

16 Linden Wrap

22 Fox in Socks

1

28 Dancing Bamboo Socks

32 Haramaki Belly Warmer

2

38 Happy Hour Cappy

42 The Ol' Pappy Cappy

46 Drunken Sweater

50 Weaving Way Socks

54 Tie-One-On Scarf

58 Barfly Pullover

62 Ruff Neck Warmer

66 Fizzy Sweater

70 Absinthe Sweater

3

78 Don't Forget Your Mittens!

82 Raspberry Wheat Ale Messenger Bag

88 Sideways Scarf

90 Slouchy Hat

94 Two-Fisted Tank

98 College Colors Cozies

100 Drink-Like-a-Fish Cozy

104 Wine Bottle Sweater

108 Dishrag Trio

112 Snakebite Hats

116 Six-Pack Carrier

120 Cherry Cordial Cardi

124 Zori Coasters

4

128 K.I.S.S. Leg Warmers, Cowl and Arm Warmers

134 Wine Charms

138 Hangover Lap Blanket

142 Whiskey Sour Messenger Bag

146 KNITTING RESOURCES

148 YARN WEIGHT GUIDELINES

149 FINISHING

149 CARING FOR YOUR HANDKNITS

150 SPECIAL TECHNIQUES GLOSSARY

154 CONTRIBUTORS

158 RESOURCES

159 INDEX

An Introduction to
SOCIAL KNITTING

Ever since knitting made its roaring comeback, people have been amazed by its meditative, relaxing and calming properties. But some time ago, we got to thinking that maybe our knitting was bored. Maybe it didn't want to just be knit quietly on the couch, on the bus or in the coffee shop.

Our knitting needed to get out of the house and go a little wild. So we decided to give our projects a night on the town. We headed to our favorite bar, ordered a round of drinks and started stitching away. We got a few odd looks, but we figured out that knitting, friends and beer is an unbeatable combination. We've been knitting socially ever since.

If you're ready to jump into social knitting, indulge in these fun, funky and portable patterns. Stylish sweaters, like the *Absinthe* and *Barfly* pullovers (pages 70 and 58, respectively) and the *Cherry Cordial Cardi* (page 120), mingle with kitschy (but still functional) projects, including beer and wine cozies (pages 98, 100 and 104), wine charms (page 134) and even a *Six-Pack Carrier* (page 116). An array of clever accessories, including the *Ruff Neck Warmer* (page 62), a hat-and-scarf-in-one

(page 112) and multiple sock patterns (pages 22, 28 and 50), round out this collection of designs for social knitting.

We're throwing the axiom "Friends don't let friends knit drunk" right out the door. If you're worried about your ability to socialize and knit at the same time, don't be. The projects in this book are helpfully rated from "Designated Driver" (tough one, better stay sober) to "Four Drinks" (easy—go on, have another!). Even if you're not a drinker, think of the project ratings as a way to measure your level of distraction. For instance, a "One Drink" project would be a better choice for watching a subtitled movie than a "Designated Driver" pattern. A new knitter might fare better with a "Three Drink" pattern than a "Designated Driver" project.

By combining some unique ideas with a sense of humor and truly talented designers, we think we have a little something here for every kind of knitter. We've also included some tips for fixing mistakes and removing stains, which will come in handy when you're knitting in a social situation. So grab your knitting bag and your buddies, and head out on the town for some social knitting. While you're at it, knit a row for us, too.

What Is
SOCIAL KNITTING?

From Karida...

Famous knitting maverick Elizabeth Zimmerman was known to knit while riding on the back of her husband's motorcycle. While Elizabeth's motorcycle knitting wasn't really a social activity, it certainly went outside the expected norms of knitting locations. Social knitting embraces the same spirit of not wanting to put down the needles. The projects in this book invite you to honestly assess your skills and level of distraction. Plus the handy sidebars give you all the tips and tricks you need to fix mistakes, clean spills and try a few new techniques. Social knitting isn't about going out and getting so drunk you spill a whole bottle of wine on your garter stitch scarf. It's about getting together with a group of friends to enjoy each other's company and work on a project you love. It's about being so excited about your knitting that you're not willing to leave it at home on bar night. So find a good venue, pack up your knitting bag (see page 26) and go be social.

A Knitting-Friendly Bar

From Libby...

We advocate knitting in all kinds of places not previously thought of as knit-friendly. That doesn't mean you can just whip out your needles anywhere, though! Not all bars are good knittin' bars. Here are some things to consider when you're picking out a bar for your Pints and Purls night.

Lighting. This might be the most important thing. Some bars are just too dark. If a bar is perfect in every way except for the lighting, ask them if you can bring in candles or a portable light for your table. Our bar in Washington, DC, has a very knit-friendly bartender, and he put a higher wattage bulb over our regular table just for us. No matter how you do it, make sure you've got enough light.

Timing. Are you planning to knit in a sports bar on football day? In a rock bar on a night when they usually have a band? Be careful with this. You need to count on always getting a table. Plus, a crowded bar means you're a lot more likely to have a random drunk fall over and land on your table.

The Crowd. When people see you knitting in a bar, they will be curious and interested. People may come up to you and ask you about it and want to chat with you. So you want to pick a bar where you're comfortable with the crowd.

Beware of the Singles Bar! If you're a woman, believe me, some men will consider the fact that you're knitting a window to hitting on you. "What are you doing there? Ohhhh, knitting! Well, my mom knits. Yeah! She knits a lot. That is real interesting that you knit. You usually think of, like, older women knitting, you know? That's cool. What are you making?" And so on. If you're lookin' for love, then maybe this isn't a bad thing. But if knitting night is supposed to be your catch-up-with-the-girls night, then don't pick the hook-up hot spot.

Volume. It can't be too loud to chat!

The main thing, though, is that you like the place. Essentially, you're looking for your personal Cheers.

Drink Ratings

You don't want to try knitting a complicated lace pattern in a noisy, dimly lit bar. But if you're getting dragged to a really boring party, you may want to take a more intricate project with you to keep yourself entertained. It's obvious that your projects need to match your skill level as well as your level of intoxication/distraction. But how do you know if a project is appropriate?

Fear not. We've got you covered. Each pattern in this book has a "drink rating" to guide you in choosing the right pattern for every situation. These little icons represent the number of beers you can have without screwing up a particular project. They're also useful to gauge your skill level—a beginner might be better off with a four-drink project than a designated-driver project. As you begin flipping through the book, you'll notice we've put the Designated Driver projects first (after all, sobriety should have some kind of reward, shouldn't it?), followed by patterns in ascending drink order so that the easiest projects are last. Use the drink rating as your handy guide, and you'll never end up stuck with the wrong knitting for the night.

DESIGNATED DRIVER *ADVANCED*
Don't mix these with whiskey.

1 DRINK *SKILLED*
Don't get distracted!

2 DRINKS *INTERMEDIATE*
You'll have to focus at least part of the time.

3 DRINKS *PRETTY EASY*
You may have to concentrate a little bit.

4 DRINKS *WAY EASY*
Minimal level of concentration and skill.

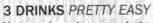

Linden Wrap

By Danielle Romanetti

The designer's passion for organic fibers and her love of entrelac knitting inspired *Linden*. This unique wrap is named after the linden tree, whose heart-shaped leaves can be seen in the pattern's lace leaf motif. It is worked in a silk and organic merino fiber from The Fibre Company, and the subtle color variation and sheen complement the entrelac pattern.

FINISHED MEASUREMENTS
Scarf: 10" wide × 60" long (25cm × 152cm)
Wrap: 20" wide × 60" long (51cm × 152cm)
Note: Pattern for wrap (pictured at left) is shown in parentheses.

YARN
5 (10) skeins The Fibre Company Organik (organic wool/silk/alpaca blend, 85 yds [78m] per 50g skein)
►►► *color* JUNGLE

NEEDLES
size US 8 (5mm) straight needles (or circular, if preferred)

NOTIONS
yarn needle

GAUGE
16 sts and 20 rows = 4" (10cm) in St st

LT (left twist): Knit through the back loop of the second st on the left needle and leaving the st on the needle, knit through the front of the first st on the left needle and slip off both sts.

RT (right twist): Knit 2 sts tog, but do not slip them off the left needle. Insert the right needle between the 2 sts and knit through the front of the first st again.

P2tog (purl 2 together): Dec 1 st by purling 2 sts tog.

KFB (knit 1 front and back): Inc 1 st by knitting into the front and back of the next st.

M1 (make 1): Inc 1 st by picking up the bar between the next st and the st just knit and knitting into it.

Sl marker or sl st(s) (slip marker or slip stitch[es]): Slip a st or sts purlwise from the left needle to the right needle. When slipping a marker, knit the sts before and after it as usual.

SSK (slip, slip, knit): Dec 1 st by slipping 2 sts knitwise one at a time, inserting the tip of the left needle into both sts and knitting the 2 sts tog.

K2tog (knit 2 together): Dec 1 st by knitting 2 sts tog.

YO (yarn over): Wrap the working yarn around the needle clockwise, and knit the next st as usual. This operation creates an eyelet hole in the knitting and inc 1 st.

Psso (pass slipped stitch over): Pass the slipped st over the st(s) just knit and off the needle, just as for binding off, to create a left-slanting decrease.

Notes:
The pattern for the wrap is given in parentheses.
Work the base triangles, followed by left-side triangle, tier 1, right-side triangle and tier 2. Cont to work left-side triangles, tier 1, right-side triangle and then tier 2 until desired length. End with 1 more tier 1 section and a right-side triangle, followed by final-tier triangles.

BASE TRIANGLES

CO 28 (56) sts.

Row 1 (RS): K1, turn.

Row 2 (and all WS rows): Purl all sts in that section, turn.

Row 3: Sl 1, k1, turn.

Row 5: Sl 1, k2, turn.

Row 7: Sl 1, k3, turn.

Row 9: Sl 1, k4, turn.

Row 11: Sl 1, k5, turn.

Row 13: Sl 1, k1, LT, k3, turn.

Row 15: Sl 1, k2, LT, k3, turn.

Row 17: Sl 1, k3, LT, k3, turn.

Row 19: Sl 1, k4, LT, k1, RT, turn.

Row 21: Sl 1, k5, LT, k3, turn.

Row 23: Sl 1, k11, turn.

Row 25: Sl 1, k12, turn.

Row 27: Sl 1, k13, do not turn.

Rep Rows 1–27 to end of row, turn.

LEFT-SIDE TRIANGLES

Row 1 (WS): K1, turn.

Row 2: KFB, turn.

Row 3: K1, p2tog, turn.

Row 4: K1, M1, k1, turn.

Row 5 (and all WS rows): K1, purl to last st in this section, purl last st and first st of next section tog, turn.

Row 6: K2, M1, k1, turn.

Row 8: K3, M1, k1, turn.

Row 10: K4, M1, k1, turn.

Row 12: K5, M1, k1, turn.

Row 14: K1, LT, k3, M1, k1, turn.

Row 16: K2, LT, k3, M1, k1, turn.

Chart 1

Key

\	SSK
/	k2tog on RS, p2tog on WS
S	slip one
◿	left twist
◺	right twist
□	knit on RS, purl on WS
0	yarn over

Row 18: K3, LT, k3, M1, k1, turn.

Row 20: K4, LT, k1, RT, M1, k1, turn.

Row 22: K5, LT, k3, M1, k1, turn.

Row 24: K11, M1, k1, turn.

Row 26: K12, M1, k1, turn.

Row 27: K1, p12, p2tog, do not turn.

TIER 1

Begin Chart 1 with Row 1 (a WS row), working all odd rows on chart from left to right and all even rows (RS rows) from right to left or foll instructions below:

Row 1 (WS): Pick up and purl 14 sts along selvedge of next triangle (or rectangle on subsequent tiers). Sl last st picked up onto left needle and p2tog, turn.

Row 2: K14, turn.

Row 3 (and all WS rows): Sl 1, p12, p2tog, turn.

Row 4: K14, turn.

Row 6: K4, k2tog, yo, k1, yo, SSK, k5, turn.

Row 8: K3, k2tog, k1, yo, k1, yo, k1, SSK, k4, turn.

Row 10: K2, k2tog, k2, yo, k1, yo, k2, SSK, k3, turn.

Row 12: K1, k2tog, k3, yo, k1, yo, k3, SSK, k2, turn.

Row 14: K1, LT, k7, RT, k2, turn.

Row 16: K2, LT, k5, RT, k3, turn.

Row 18: K3, LT, k3, RT, k4, turn.

Row 20: K4, LT, k1, RT, k5, turn.

Row 22: K5, LT, k7, turn.

Row 24: K14, turn.

Row 26: K14, turn.

Row 27: Sl 1, p12, p2tog, do not turn.

Rep Rows 1–27 across.

RIGHT-SIDE TRIANGLES

Row 1 (WS): Pick up and purl 14 sts along selvedge of last triangle (or rectangle on subsequent tiers), turn.

Row 2: Knit, turn.

Row 3 (and all WS rows): Sl 1, purl to last 2 sts, k2tog, turn.

Row 4: Knit, turn.

Row 6: K2, k2tog, yo, k1, yo, SSK, k5, turn.

Row 8: K4, yo, k1, SSK, k4, turn.

Row 10: K3, yo, k2, SSK, k3, turn.

Row 12: K2, yo, k3, SSK, k2, turn.

Row 14: K4, RT, k2, turn.

Row 16: K2, RT, k3, turn.

Row 18: K6, turn.

Row 20: K5, turn.

Row 22: K4, turn.

Row 24: K3, turn.

Row 26: K2, turn.

Row 27: K2tog, the rem st will be counted as the first st picked up for the first rectangle in the next tier. Turn and transfer this st to the right needle.

TIER 2

Begin Chart 2 (page 21) or foll instructions below:

Row 1 (RS): With RS facing, pick up and knit 14 sts along selvedge of next rectangle or triangle. For the first rectangle only, the rem st from the last tier counts as 1 picked up st. Sl last st picked up to left needle and SSK, turn.

Row 2 (and all WS rows): P14, turn.

Row 3: Sl 1, k12, SSK, turn.

Row 5: Sl 1, k12, SSK, turn.

Row 7: Sl 1, k4, k2tog, yo, k1, yo, SSK, k3, SSK, turn.

Row 9: Sl 1, k3, k2tog, k1, yo, k1, yo, k1, SSK, k2, SSK, turn.

Row 11: Sl 1, k2, k2tog, k2, yo, k1, yo, k2, SSK, k1, SSK, turn.

Row 13: Sl 1, k1, k2tog, k3, yo, k1, yo, k3, SSK, SSK, turn.

Row 15: Sl 1, k1, LT, k7, RT, SSK, turn.

Row 17: Sl 1, k2, LT, k5, RT, k1, SSK, turn.

Row 19: Sl 1, k3, LT, k3, RT, k2, SSK, turn.

Row 21: Sl 1, k4, LT, k1, RT, k3, SSK, turn.

Row 23: Sl 1, k6, RT, k4, SSK, turn.

Row 25: Sl 1, k12, SSK, turn.

Row 27: Sl 1, k12, SSK. Do not turn.

Rep Rows 1–27 across.

Rep from left-side triangle until piece measures approx 58" (147cm), ending with left-side triangle, tier 1, right-side triangle.

FINAL TIER TRIANGLES

Row 1 (RS): With RS facing, pick up and knit 14 sts along selvedge of next rectangle or triangle. For the first triangle only, the st rem from the last section counts as the first picked-up st. Sl last st picked up to left needle and SSK, turn.

Row 2 (and all WS rows): Purl to the end of sts in the section, turn.

Row 3: K2tog, k11, SSK, turn.

Row 5: K2tog, k10, SSK, turn.

Row 7: K2tog, k1, k2tog, yo, k1, yo, SSK, k3, SSK, turn.

Row 9: K2tog, k3, yo, k1, SSK, k2, SSK, turn.

Row 11: K2tog, k2, yo, k2, SSK, k1, SSK, turn.

Row 13: K2tog, k1, yo, k3, SSK, SSK, turn.

Row 15: K2tog, k3, RT, SSK, turn.

Row 17: K2tog, k1, RT, k1, SSK, turn.

Row 19: K2tog, k3, SSK, turn.

Row 21: K2tog, k2, SSK, turn.

Row 23: K2tog, k1, SSK, turn.

Row 25: K2tog, SSK, turn.

Row 27: Sl 1, SSK, psso, do not turn. The rem st will count as first st picked up for the next triangle. When all triangles have been worked, BO the last st.

Rep Rows 1–27 across.

FINISHING

Weave in ends. Block firmly. If desired, add fringe to ends or tassels to corners, as shown.

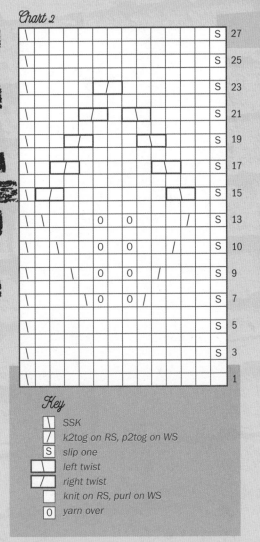

Chart 2

Key

\\	SSK
/	k2tog on RS, p2tog on WS
S	slip one
☐ (left twist)	left twist
☐ (right twist)	right twist
☐	knit on RS, purl on WS
0	yarn over

A Word about Charts

From Libby...

Do not be afraid of charts. Charts are just misunderstood. They are that girl in high school who seems prickly and a little intimidating, but then you are forced to be science partners with her, and it turns out that she is really cool and also good at science.

Charts show you a knitting pattern visually. The tricky thing about them is that they mirror the physical knitting. Got that? Because it is way important. A chart represents the right side of a piece of knitted fabric, with each box representing a stitch. Here is how to read them. If it seems a little backwards to you, you are not alone, but I promise that after you do it, it will all make sense.

Always read a chart from bottom to top. Read a chart from right to left on the Right Side. Read it from left to right on the Wrong Side.

Again, the chart mirrors the knitting, so you read it back and forth, just like you knit. If you're knitting in the round, however, you always read the chart from right to left, because you're always knitting on the Right Side.

Fox in Socks

By Kathleen Lawton—Trask

So you're the designated driver. Or you're on antibiotics, or in a twelve-step program, or just don't feel like imbibing tonight. Well, this is your lucky night, because you get to show off your knitting skills while all around you knitters are doing shots every time they drop a stitch and trying to dunk their half-finished scarves in their beer chasers. Rejoice! You have your dignity! And you have these nice Fair Isle socks, based on a mitten pattern from Robin Hansen's *Fox & Geese & Fences*, to prove you're the most talented (not to mention the most sober) gal in the room.

SIZES
Child (Woman, Man)

FINISHED MEASUREMENTS
6 (7½, 9)" (15 [19, 23]cm)
foot circumference

YARN
1 (2, 2) skeins Neighborhood Fiber Co. Studio Sport (wool, 127 yds [116m] per 57g skein)
►►► *color* GRANT CIRCLE (A)
1 (2, 2) skeins Neighborhood Fiber Co. Studio Sport
►►► *color* SHERIDAN CIRCLE (B)

Note: If you decide to knit both socks the same way, you may need more of color B.

NEEDLES
1 set of 4 size US 4 (3.5mm) DPNs
1 set of 4 size US 3 (3.25mm) DPNs

NOTIONS
2 locking stitch markers
yarn needle

GAUGE
32 sts and 32 rows = 4" (10cm) in patt st using larger needles

DESIGNATED DRIVER

LEG

With larger needles and B, loosely CO 48 (60, 72) sts. Arrange as foll:

Needle 1: 12 (15, 18) sts.

Needle 2: 24 (30, 36) sts.

Needle 3: 12 (15, 18) sts.

Rep chart (below) a total of 8 (9, 10) times or to desired leg length, ending with Rnd 6. Congratulate yourself! By now, the drunken idiots around you are either hiding their knitting in their purses because they have made so many errors they cannot bear to have anyone see it, or they are forging boldly ahead, though their scarves are quickly turning into shawls.

HEEL FLAP

Move needle 1 sts onto needle 3, and switch to smaller needles and A. Working on 24 (30, 36) sts for heel, leaving instep sts on hold, cont as foll:

Row 1 (RS): *Sl 1, k1; rep from * to end of row.

Row 2: Sl 1, purl to end of row.

Rep Rows 1–2 a total of 11 (14, 17) times.

Chart

17
15
13
11
9
7
5
3
1

17   15   13   11   9   7   5   3   1

Key

color A
color B

24

TURN HEEL

Row 1: Sl 1, k13 (17, 20), k2tog, k1, turn.

Row 2: Sl 1, p5 (7, 7), p2tog, p1, turn.

Row 3: Sl 1, knit to 1 st before gap, k2tog over gap, k1, turn.

Row 4: Sl 1, purl to 1 st before gap, p2tog over gap, p1, turn.

Rep Rows 3–4 until all sts have been worked—14 (16, 22) sts.

GUSSET

At this point, the drunks are asking you to drive them home. Tell them you've reached a critical point in the creation of your sock, and pass them the mixed nuts on the bar. They can probably use the salt.

Change to B. Knit 1 plain row across bottom of heel. Using the same needle (needle 1), pick up and knit 11 (14, 17) sts on the side of the heel flap, pick up and knit 1 st between heel flap and instep (place marker in this st). With needle 2, work in k2, p2 ribbing across instep sts. With needle 3, pick up and knit another st between instep and heel flap, and place marker in this st. Then pick up and knit 11 (14, 17) sts down the opposite side of the heel flap. Knit 7 (8, 11) of the heel sts onto needle 3. The back of the heel marks the new beg of the rnd.

Note:
On the next rnd, knit the marked sts through the back loop, then remove the markers.

Rnd 1:

Needle 1: Knit to last 3 sts, k2tog, k1.

Needle 2: (P2, k2) across.

Needle 3: K1, SSK, knit to end.

Rnd 2:

Needle 1: Knit to end.

Needle 2: (P2, k2) across.

Needle 3: Knit to end.

Rep Rnds 1–2 until there are 48 (60, 72) sts.

FOOT

Work even in patt until foot measures 5 (8, 9)" (13 [20, 23]cm) or approx 1½ (2, 2½)" (4 [5, 6]cm) less than desired foot length.

You're almost there! By this time you probably really do have to drive the idiots home. Don't let any of them go home with unsavory characters, not even if they tell you they've found their soul mates. Not even if you're really annoyed with them. Just put the sock into your bag, drive them home, then go home, get some sleep, wake up and do your toe.

TOE

Change to A.

Rnd 1:

Needle 1: Knit to last 3 sts, k2tog, k1.

Needle 2: K1, SSK, knit to last 3 sts, k2tog, k1.

Needle 3: K1, SSK, knit to end.

Rnd 2: Knit.

Rep Rnds 1–2 until 12 (16, 20) sts rem.

Graft sts together using Kitchener st. You're done!

Now you just have 1 more sock to go. For the next sock, reverse the color patt to keep yourself awake and to use the same amount of yarn in each color.

FINISHING

Weave in ends.

Libby's
NOTIONS BAG

Karida's
NOTIONS BAG

Libby's Notions Bag

When you start treating the bar as knitting central as well as party central, you need to put your notions bag in the essentials category along with your lip gloss, ID and cell phone. Get yourself a fun, little pouch—the ones pictured are by Lexie Barnes—and fill 'er up.

The Essentials:

► crochet hook
► tape measure
► stitch markers
► cable needles or DPNs
► stitch holders
► yarn needle
► scrap yarn
► pen
► wine bottle opener

My bag also contains a needle gauge, little scissors, some Burt's Bees hand creme, some safety pins and a highlighter. Some Wetnaps wouldn't hurt either (don't pretend you don't want some fries). Adopt the Boy Scout motto, because anything could happen.

Karida's Notions Bag

Libby and I are in total agreement on the importance of your notions bag. I like to think of my notions bag as a "Just-in-Case" bag. Just in case I drop a bunch of stitches. Just in case I completely screw up the lace repeat. Because I've done these things. And many, many others.

The Essentials:

► 2 crochet hooks—size A for picking up smaller stitches and size F for larger stuff
► spare cable needle (once you've dropped a cable needle on the bar floor under the booth, you don't really want to use it again that night)
► smooth, light-colored waste yarn for if I screw up a WIP and know I'll need to fix it at home later (just thread a darning needle and slip it through the live stitches, leaving them on hold for later)
► tiny flashlight (Maglite makes lots of neat small flashlights)
► Wetnaps, because I know I'm going to want some French fries and possibly a sandwich
► stain removal pen or wipes (with stains, quick response is key—see Don't Cry Over Spilled Beer, page 119)
► darning needles
► stitch markers
► yarn cutter or scissors
► needle gauge
► tape measure
► pencil

Dancing Bamboo Socks

By Holly Daymude

You might think lace would be too complicated to knit at the bar. But this simple pattern is easy to memorize and fairly repetitive. Knit from the cuff down, these socks use basic construction and an easy pattern stitch to create a sock that any knitter can tackle.

SIZES
women's—customizable

FINISHED MEASUREMENTS
8" (20cm) foot circumference

YARN
1 skein C*Eye*Ber Fiber Merino Tencel Fingering Weight (superwash merino/Tencel blend, 410 yds [375m] per 114g skein)
►►► color CRIMSON AND CLOVER

NEEDLES
2 24" (61cm) size US 1 (2.5mm) circular needles

NOTIONS
stitch markers
yarn needle

GAUGE
32 sts and 40 rows = 4" (10cm) in St st

YO (yarn over): Wrap the working yarn around the needle clockwise, and knit the next st as usual. This operation creates an eyelet hole in the knitting and inc 1 st.

SSK (slip, slip, knit): Dec 1 st by slipping 2 sts knitwise 1 at a time, inserting the tip of the left needle into both sts and knitting the 2 sts tog.

P2tog (purl 2 together): Dec 1 st by purling 2 sts tog.

K2tog (knit 2 together): Dec 1 st by knitting 2 sts tog.

Bamboo Chart

−	\	0				−		9
−		\	0			−		7
−			\	0		−		5
−			\	0		−		3
−				\	0	−		1

Note: Even-numbered rows are not charted. Work even-numbered rows in pattern as established.

Key

\	SSK
	knit
−	purl
0	yarn over

LEG

CO 64 sts. Divide sts evenly over both needles.

Pm and join, being careful not to twist.

Work in k2, p2 ribbing for 1" (3cm).

Set-Up Rnd: *P1, k6, p1; rep from * around.

BAMBOO PATTERN

Work bamboo patt as foll below or using the chart on page 30.

Rnd 1: *P1, yo, SSK, k4, p1; rep from * around.

Rnd 2 (and all even rnds to 10): *P1, k6, p1; rep from * around.

Rnd 3: *P1, k1, yo, SSK, k3, p1; rep from * around.

Rnd 5: *P1, k2, yo, SSK, k2, p1; rep from * around.

Rnd 7: *P1, k3, yo, SSK, k1, p1; rep from * around.

Rnd 9: *P1, k4, yo, SSK, p1; rep from * around.

Rep Rnds 1–10 until leg measures 10" (25cm) or desired length, ending with Rnd 10.

HEEL FLAP

Working on 32 sts for heel, leaving instep sts on hold, cont as foll:

Row 1 (RS): *Sl 1, k1; rep from * to end of row.

Row 2: *Sl 1, purl to end of row.

Rep Rows 1–2 a total of 14 times.

TURN HEEL

Row 1: K18, SSK, k1, turn.

Row 2: Sl 1, p5, p2tog, p1, turn.

Row 3: Sl 1, k6, SSK, k1, turn.

Row 4: Sl 1, p7, p2tog, p1, turn.

Cont shaping the heel in this manner, working 1 more st before each dec, ending with:

Row 13: K16, SSK, k1, turn.

Row 14: P17, p2tog, p1, turn—18 sts.

GUSSET

Knit across the 18 heel sts.

Using the same needle, pick up 14 sts along the heel flap (1 st in each slipped st along the flap), make 1 additional st in the space between the gusset and the instep sts.

Using the 2nd needle, work in patt across the instep sts.

Using the 1st needle again, make 1 st in the space between the instep and gusset, pick up 14 sts along the heel flap.

K9 heel sts, pm to mark new start of rnd.

Rnd 1: K9 sts, knit rem heel sts tbl to the last 2 sts, k2tog. Work in patt across the instep. SSK, knit rem heel sts tbl to the last 9 sts, k9.

Rnd 2: Knit.

Rep Rnds 1–2 until there are 64 sts.

FOOT

Cont in patt across the instep and in St st across the sole with no additional dec until sock measures approx 2" (5cm) less than desired length.

Set-Up Rnd: Knit.

TOE

Rnd 1: *K1, SSK, knit to last 3 sts on the 1st needle, k2tog, k1; rep from * once more on 2nd needle.

Rnd 2: Knit.

Rep Rnds 1–2 until there are 24 sts.

Graft the sts tog using Kitchener st.

Rep to make a second sock.

FINISHING

Weave in ends.

Haramaki Belly Warmer

By Olga Buraya-Kefelian

The belly warmer dates back centuries to the Land of the Rising Sun and the culture of the East. In Japanese tradition, body heat is known to be centered around one's abdomen, so people have long worn belly warmers to fight cold, snowy winters. Recently, this ancient tradition has made a comeback. *Haramaki* can be worn on top of your jeans or on top of a dress to emphasize the waist. Or it can be pulled up or shifted down on your hips. This belt is worked sideways, utilizing short rows to create a zigzag pattern and grafted afterwards to join.

FINISHED MEASUREMENTS
18 (21, 24, 30, 33, 39, 45)" (46 [53, 61, 76, 84, 99, 114]cm)

SIZES
To fit 23 (25, 28, 32, 37, 43, 48)" (58 [64, 71, 81, 94, 109, 122]cm) waist

YARN
1 (1, 1, 1, 2, 2, 2) skein(s) Neighborhood Fiber Co. Watershed (merino/Seacell blend, 354 yds [324m] per 114g skein)
►►► *color* LOGAN CIRCLE (A)
1 (1, 1, 1, 2, 2, 2) skein(s) Neighborhood Fiber Co. Watershed
►►► *color* WASHINGTON CIRCLE (B)

NEEDLES
size US 4 (3.5mm) straight needles

NOTIONS
waste yarn
yarn needle

GAUGE
26 sts and 48 rows = 4" (10cm) in garter st

BELT

Using a provisional method and waste yarn, CO 52 sts.

Starting with B and RS facing, work foll the chart (opposite page). Work 1st section in B, foll short row patt, then join A at beg with WS facing and work A section, then join B with RS facing and work 2nd B section.

Rep the chart a total of 6 (7, 8, 10, 11, 13, 15) times—18 (21, 24, 30, 33, 39, 45)" (46 [53, 61, 76, 84, 99, 114]cm). Do not BO.

FINISHING

Unravel provisional cast on and place sts on a separate needle. Graft the 2 ends tog using Kitchener st.

Weave in ends. Wash and block as desired.

The Knitting Support Group

From Libby...

Nothing is worse than knitting happily along on a project only to suddenly realize you've screwed up terribly and you need to frog it. Sometimes, when this happens to me, I just can't face the frogging, and the project ends up sitting sadly in my knitting basket until I can build up the courage to fix it.

When this happens, I usually take the project to my knitting group at my favorite bar. The moral support of four or five really good knitters who are not emotionally invested in the project gives me a less doom-and-gloom feeling about the whole thing. If I can't face the horror of tearing out all those pretty stitches, I can hand it over to a friend and ask her to please rip it back for me. A few minutes later the painful part is done, and I am back on my merry way.

Plus, if I bring the messed-up project, and only the messed-up project to knit night, I will be forced to work on it, because you know I can't stand to just sit there and not knit while everyone else is knitting.

Chart

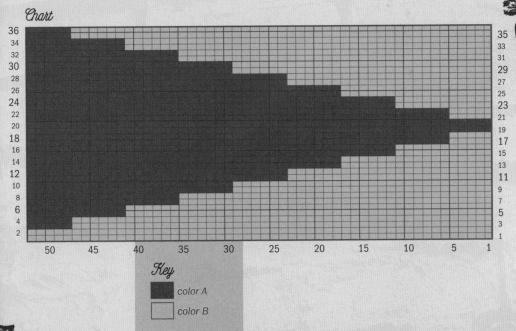

Key

- ■ color A
- □ color B

Oops, You Did it Again

From Libby...

If you're not paying full attention to your knitting, you may make a mistake. That's just life. Luckily, mistakes are not permanent in knitting. You can always fix the mistake, whatever it may be. Here are a few quick lessons in cleaning up after yourself.

Fixing Dropped Stitches

Losing one stitch is definitely a pain, but there is nothing quite like looking down at your project and seeing a sad skeletal ladder—a whole crop of dropped stitches. If this happens to you, do not panic. Secure all stitches with a DPN, straw, stick, scrap yarn—whatever you've got. Your first priority is to make sure those suckers don't drop down any farther. Once they're solid, get your crochet hook.

Then you're just a few simple steps away from fixing that dropped stitch.

1. Pick up the first stitch—if it is a knit stitch, you will stick your crochet hook in front to back, with the bottommost ladder rung behind it.

2. Grab that ladder rung with your hook, and pull it through the stitch from back to front. See that tidy knit stitch? Nice!

3. Keep your hook in there and grab the next ladder rung. Pull that one through, too. Keep going until your little stitch is back on top. Sit him on the needle.

If you are so fortunate as to have only dropped one stitch, then drink a toast, 'cause you're back on track! If you have dropped multiple stitches, go back to the bottom and the next dropped stitch, and repeat this process until all your little runaways are back on the needle.

Tip: Picking up Purls

It is a little tricky to pick up dropped purl stitches, so I often flip the knitting over and pick them up knitwise on the wrong side.

Changing Knits into Purls

If you notice ten rows too late that you knitted a purl or purled a knit, there is no need to rip all the way back. Just knit to the stitch directly above the mistake, drop the stitch all the way down, stopping when you've unraveled the offending stitch. Then use your crochet hook to pick up the little ladder rungs from back to front to make knits, or from front to back to make purls.

Baby Rips Back

Whoops! Accidental yarn over? Forget to increase? Try as you might to avoid it, sometimes you just have to rip back your knitting. Sure, it's a little scary. Calm yourself—deep breathing, glass of wine. Now. Pull out the needle. All at once. Like it's a Band-Aid. Unravel until the mistake is gone. *Voilà!* A clean slate. Now you need to put those stitches back on the needle, and you need to do it right. (It's not life or death—if you put them on backwards, the worst that will happen is you will have one row of twisted stitches, which looks a little funny.) I just stick 'em back on the needle and carry on knitting. When I get to a backwards stitch, I just knit it through the back loop, which corrects the twist.

Happy Hour Cappy

By Libby Bruce

If you are grumpy and bummed out because it's the stupid, cold, wet winter, I would recommend meeting your knitters at a bar with good happy hour pricing. While you're there, you can spend time knitting some warm, soft wool into a bright hat in springtime colors. This hat is simple, but the mini cables make it an interesting knit. And since it's made from Mission Falls 1824 Wool, this hat is not only soft and warm and pretty, it is also tough as nails, so no worries about wearing it in the worst winter weather.

FINISHED MEASUREMENTS
Hat circumference: 21" (53cm)

YARN
1 skein Mission Falls 1824 Wool
(100% wool, 85 yds [78m] per 50g
skein) in each of the foll colors:
▶▶▶ *color #024 DAMSON (A)*
▶▶▶ *color #030 TEAL (B)*
▶▶▶ *color #026 ZINNIA (C)*
▶▶▶ *color #532 BASIL (D)*

NEEDLES
16" (41cm) size US 8 (5mm)
circular needle
1 set of 5 size US 8 (5mm) DPNs

NOTIONS
stitch marker
yarn needle

GAUGE
18 sts and 20 rows = 4" (10cm)
in patt st

BABY CABLE

Rnds 1–3: *K2, p2; rep from * around.

Rnd 4: *K2tog, leave on left needle. Insert right needle back into first st on needle, k1, drop all sts just knitted, p2; rep from * around.

Rep Rnds 1–4.

HAT

With circular needle and B, CO 96 sts. Pm and join, being careful not to twist. Working in Baby Cable patt, change colors as foll:

Rnds 1–4: Color B.

Rnds 5–8: Color D.

Rnds 9–12: Color A.

Rnds 13–16: Color C.

Rep Rnds 1–16.

Work even as est until piece measures 6" (15cm) from beg. Cont in stripe patt, dec for crown, changing to DPNs when needed.

DECREASE ROUNDS

Rnd 1: *K2, p2, k2, p2tog; rep from * around— 84 sts.

Rnd 2: *K2, p2, k2, p1; rep from * around.

Rnd 3: *K2, p2tog, k2, p1; rep from * around— 72 sts.

Rnd 4: *K2tog, p1; rep from * around—48 sts.

Rnd 5: *K2tog; rep from * around—24 sts.

Rnd 6: Knit.

Rnd 7: *K2tog; rep from * around—12 sts.

Rnd 8: Knit.

Rnd 9: *K2tog; rep from * around—6 sts.

Break yarn. Thread tail through rem 6 sts, fasten off.

FINISHING

Weave in ends.

Don't Fear The Beer

From Libby...

You have to have the right frame of mind if you are going to knit in the bar. The patterns in this book are designed to be beer-and-knitter-friendly. Here, though, is a grim, inescapable fact: Alcohol facilitates mistakes. You will drop a stitch. You will knit the wrong row of your pattern. You'll forget to increase.

You need to be able to face down a dropped stitch with an icy capability befitting a German nanny. You need to be able to look down, laugh and say, "I totally screwed this up. Someone get me a beer." Here is an important thing to remember for the whole rest of your life: In knitting, no mistake is permanent.

The Ol' Pappy Cappy

By Libby Bruce

This hat was inspired by my good friend, the Ol' Pappy, who is an unshakable devotee of neutral colors and who likes to stay warm and stylish while he drinks his PBR. It's an easy, versatile, functional hat with hipster flair. You can really play with this pattern. If you're not into floppy earflaps, you could make them wider and shorter by picking up more stitches and starting the decreases earlier. In fact, you could leave off the earflaps altogether (just be sure to add about an inch [three centimeters] to the length before you decrease). I wouldn't recommend this, though, because earflaps are awesome.

FINISHED MEASUREMENTS

Hat circumference: stretches to fit up to 24" (61cm)
One size fits all

YARN

1 skein Mission Falls 1824 Wool (100% wool, 85 yds [78m] per 50g skein) in each of the foll colors:
▶▶▶ *color* #001 NATURAL (A)
▶▶▶ *color* #003 OYSTER (B)
▶▶▶ *color* #004 CHARCOAL (C)
▶▶▶ *color* #005 RAVEN (D)

NEEDLES

16" (41cm) size US 8 (5mm) circular needle
1 set of 5 size US 8 (5mm) DPNs

NOTIONS

stitch markers
yarn needle

GAUGE

18 sts and 20 rows = 4" (10cm) in St st

2

NOTES

Pm (place marker): Slip a premade marker or a loosely knotted piece of scrap yarn in a contrasting color onto the right needle after the st just knit to mark a spot in the knitting to refer to on future rows. When you come to a marker, simply slip it from the right-hand needle to the left-hand needle.

P2tog (purl 2 together): Dec 1 st by purling 2 sts tog.

K2tog (knit 2 together): Dec 1 st by knitting 2 sts tog.

SSK (slip, slip, knit): Dec 1 st by slipping 2 sts knitwise one at a time, inserting the tip of the left needle into both sts and knitting the 2 sts tog.

HAT

With B, CO 96 sts. Pm and join, being careful not to twist. Work in k2, p2 rib in stripe patt as foll:

Rnds 1–5: Color B.

Rnds 6–10: Color D.

Rnds 11–15: Color A.

Rnds 16–20: Color C.

Rep Rnds 1–20 until piece measures 5" (13cm) from beg.

DECREASE ROUNDS

Cont in stripe patt as est, dec for crown, changing to DPNs when needed.

Next Rnd: *K2, p2tog, k2, p2; rep from * around—84 sts.

Next Rnd: *K2, p1, k2, p2; rep from * around.

Next Rnd: *K2, p1, k2, p2tog; rep from * around—72 sts.

Next Rnd: *K2, p1; rep from * around.

Next Rnd: *K2tog, p1; rep from * around— 48 sts.

Next Rnd: *K1, p1; rep from * around.

Next Rnd: *K2tog; rep from * around—24 sts.

Next Rnd: Knit.

Rep last 2 rnds until 6 sts rem.

Break yarn. Thread tail through rem 6 sts, fasten off.

EARFLAPS

Put the hat on the head of the wearer to determine and mark the placement of the earflaps (alternately, evenly space them on opposite sides of the hat). With C, pick up and knit 18 sts. Cont in stripe patt, working in k2, p2 rib, taking care to align the knits and purls of the earflaps with the knits and purls of the hat.

Work even for 10 rows.

Next Row: SSK, work in patt to last 2 sts, k2tog.

Rep last row until 4 sts rem. BO.

Rep for other earflap.

FINISHING

Weave in ends.

Knitter's Night In

From Libby...

I love going out and being part of the mix of those special people who choose to leave their homes on a weeknight. Sometimes, though, staying in sounds better—I want to be cozy, or I want to have an intimate chat with my good friends, or I am stone-cold broke. Whatever the reason, some nights it's a better idea to have your pints and purls at someone's home.

If you're the lucky host, have a cozy spot set up, put on some music and have a quality night in. Here are some ideas to make your night a success.

Stick-in-the-Wool: The Knitter's Shot

recipe by Kristin Ritchey

Talk about delicious! This shot will get your night started off right. A word of warning: You've got to use real Pama, not the imitation stuff—it's just not as tasty.

- 2 counts Orange Vodka
- 1 count Pama
- 1 count Butterscotch Pucker
- 1 count Baileys

Bruce's Spicy Black Bean Dip

You can make this yummy dip ahead of time and just microwave it when your guests arrive. It's a great party food and a definite crowd-pleaser.

- 2 cans black beans
- half a medium onion, chopped
- 1 ripe tomato, chopped
- 1 small jalapeño pepper, chopped and seeded
- ½ cup cheddar cheese (vegans: substitute soft tofu for cheddar)
- juice of 1 lemon
- 1 large clove garlic
- salt to taste

In a food processor, puree black beans, jalapeño, cheese, lemon juice, salt and garlic. Transfer dip to a medium sauce pan and heat slowly on medium heat. Stir in onion, tomato and some of the jalapeño seeds. When dip is hot, top with a dollop of sour cream and some shredded cheddar. Serve with nacho chips.

Knit-in Swap

Knitter's night in is a great time to have a yarn swap. You know you've got some nice yarn stashed away that you'll probably never use: a leftover ball from a completed project, something you bought on a whim and can't find a use for, or the materials from an abandoned sweater. Get rid of that stuff and replace it with something you really want! Have everyone bring a few balls, then trade 'em around like baseball cards. Everyone will leave happy.

Drunken Sweater

By Olga Buraya-Kefelian

Asymmetrical clothing really draws attention. Inspired by the great clothing designer Yohji Yamamoto, this garment represents the eye-catching quality of the asymmetrical look. Less is more, so this minimalistic sweater is worked in the round in simple Stockinette stitch with shifted sleeves and a prominent collar. The details of this sweater make it a great garment for the weekend—or for any time.

SIZES
Women's XS (S, M, L, XL, XXL)

FINISHED MEASUREMENTS
Bust: 30 (34, 38, 42, 46, 50)"
(76 [86, 97, 107, 117, 127]cm)
Length: 21 (22, 23, 24, 25, 26)"
(53 [56, 58, 61, 64, 66]cm)

YARN
6 (7, 7, 8, 9, 10) skeins Shibui Knits Merino Alpaca (baby alpaca/merino wool blend, 131 yds [120m] per 100g skein)
►►► *color #7495 WASABI*

NEEDLES
24" (61cm) size US 8 (5mm) circular needle
Note: Larger sizes may require a longer needle.
1 set of 5 size US 8 (5mm) DPNs

NOTIONS
waste yarn for holders
stitch markers
yarn needle

GAUGE
16 sts and 20 rows = 4" (10cm) in St st

2

Note: This sweater is worked circularly from the bottom up with deliberately mismatched armholes.

LOWER BODY

With circular needle, CO 120 (136, 152, 168, 184, 200) sts. Pm and join, being careful not to twist.

Purl 1 rnd, placing 2nd marker after 60 (68, 76, 84, 92, 100) sts to mark opposite side "seam."

Work even in St st until piece measures 9 (9½, 10, 10½, 11, 11½)" (23 [24, 25, 27, 28, 29]cm). Set aside.

SLEEVES (MAKE 2)

With DPNs, CO 40 (44, 48, 52, 56, 60) sts. Pm and join, being careful not to twist.

Purl 1 rnd.

Work even in St st until piece measures 11 (11, 11½, 11½, 12, 12)" (28 [28, 29, 29, 30, 30]cm).

Set 1st sleeve aside, cont to work 2nd sleeve even until piece measures 16 (16, 16½, 16½, 17, 17)" (41 [41, 42, 42, 43, 43]cm). Set aside.

UPPER BODY

On body, work to 3 (3, 3, 3, 4, 4) sts before 1st marker. Place next 6 (6, 6, 6, 8, 8) sts on holder for underarm. Pick up shorter sleeve. Place 3 (3, 3, 3, 4, 4) sts from either side of marker (6 [6, 6, 6, 8, 8] sts total) on holder from sleeve. Hold sleeve to body with held sts tog, pm, knit across rem 34 (38, 42, 46, 48, 52) sleeve sts, pm, cont to end of rnd.

Work even in St st on body sts and shorter sleeve until piece measures 4" (10cm) from point sleeve was joined.

Join 2nd sleeve on opposite side of body in same manner as first—176 (200, 224, 248, 264, 288) sts.

YOKE

On shorter sleeve, move markers to either side of center 4 sts (on outside of arm). Leave markers in place on longer sleeve. Pm at center back to mark new beg of rnd.

Work even for 1" (3cm).

SHAPE YOKE

Rnd 1: Knit.

Rnd 2: Knit to 3 sts before 1st marker of shorter sleeve, k3tog, sl marker, knit to 2nd marker, sl marker, sl 1, k2tog, psso; knit across body; on longer sleeve, *knit to 3 sts before 1st marker, k2tog, k1, sl marker, k1, SSK; rep from * at 2nd marker, knit to end—8 sts dec.

Rep Rnds 1–2 until 88 (88, 92, 96, 100, 104) sts rem.

Work even until armhole from point longer sleeve was joined measures 8 (8½, 9, 9½, 10, 10½)" (20 [22, 23, 24, 25, 27]cm).

SHAPE NECK

Work even for 1½" (4cm).

Turning Ridge for Hem: Purl 1 rnd.

Work even in St st for 1½" (4cm) more. Do not bind off.

FINISHING

Fold hem of neck opening to WS. With yarn needle, sew each live st to inside of garment to secure. Place held underarm sts on needles, join with Kitchener st.

Weave in ends. Block if needed.

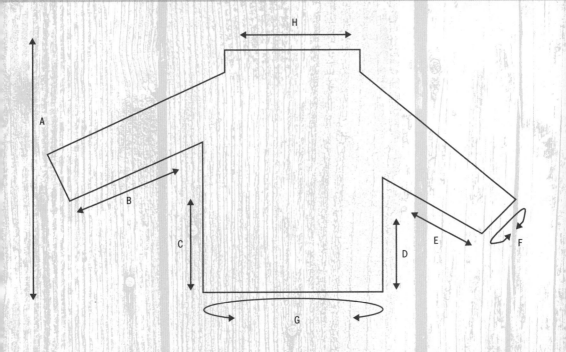

A: 21 (22, 23, 24, 25, 26)" (53 [56, 58, 61, 64, 66]cm)

B: 16 (16, 16½, 16½, 17, 17)" (41 [41, 42, 42, 43, 43]cm)

C: 13 (13½, 14, 14½, 15, 15½)" (33 [34, 36, 37, 38, 39]cm)

D: 9 (9½, 10, 10½, 11, 11½)" (23 [24, 25, 27, 28, 29]cm)

E: 11 (11, 11½, 11½, 12, 12)" (28 [28, 29, 29, 30, 30]cm)

F: 10 (11, 12, 13, 14, 15)" (25 [28, 30, 33, 36, 38]cm)

G: 30 (34, 38, 42, 46, 50)" (76 [86, 97, 107, 117, 127]cm)

H: 11 (11, 11½, 12, 12½, 13)" [28 (28, 29, 30, 32, 33) cm]

Weaving Way Socks

By Kathleen Lawton–Trask

The pattern in these simple socks mimics the meandering path folks who have been, well, over-served might take home. A knit four, purl four rib shifts one stitch over each round and changes direction every eight rounds. It sounds complicated, but the pattern is easily memorized and the stitches are easily read if you get lost.

A provisional heel makes this the perfect project for an evening of more than one drink. Best of all, if you miss a round or your pattern veers off in another direction—it will make the weaving path that much more interesting.

SIZES
Youth L/Women's S (Women's L, Men's S)

FINISHED MEASUREMENTS
7 (8½, 10)" (18 [22, 25]cm) foot circumference

YARN
2 (2, 3) skeins Neighborhood Fiber Co. Studio Worsted (wool, 98 yds [90m] per 57g skein)
►►► *color* GRANT CIRCLE

NEEDLES
2 24" (61cm) size US 4 (3.5mm) circular needles

NOTIONS
stitch markers
waste yarn
yarn needle

GAUGE
23 sts and 30 rows = 4" (10cm) in patt st

LEG

CO 40 (48, 56) sts. Divide sts evenly over both needles. Pm and join, being careful not to twist.

Rnd 1: *K4, p4; rep from * around.

Rnd 2: K3, (p4, k4) to last st, k1.

Rnd 3: K2, (p4, k4) to last 2 sts, k2.

Rnd 4: K1, (p4, k4) to last 3 sts, k3.

Rnd 5: *P4, k4; rep from * around.

Rnd 6: P3, (k4, p4) to last st, p1.

Rnd 7: P2, (k4, p4) to last 2 sts, p2.

Rnd 8: P1, (k4, p4) to last 3 sts, p3.

Rnd 9: *K4, p4; rep from * around.

Rnd 10: P1, (k4, p4) to last 3 sts, p3.

Rnd 11: P2, (k4, p4) to last 2 sts, p2.

Rnd 12: P3, (k4, p4) to last st, p1.

Rnd 13: *P4, k4; rep from * around.

Rnd 14: K1, (p4, k4) to last 3 sts, k3.

Rnd 15: K2, (p4, k4) to last 2 sts, k2.

Rnd 16: K3, (p4, k4) to last st, k1.

Rep Rnds 1–16 2 (3, 4) times more or to desired leg length.

PROVISIONAL HEEL

Drop main yarn but do not cut it. Join waste yarn and knit first 20 (24, 28) sts of next rnd with waste yarn. Cut waste yarn. Return to beg of rnd, cont in patt (knitting waste yarn sts in patt as well). Heel will be completed after you're done with the rest of the sock (and have had a nice sleep as well as some aspirin and possibly an egg sandwich).

FOOT

After putting in waste yarn for provisional heel, work 3 (4, 5) more patt rnds or approx 1½ (2, 2½)" (4 [5, 6]cm) less than desired foot length.

STAR TOE

Knit 1 rnd plain.

Rnd 1: K2, SSK, k12 (20, 28), k2tog, k2; rep on second needle.

Rnd 2: Knit.

Rep Rnds 1–2 until there are 10 (12, 14) sts left on each needle. Then work Rnd 1 every rnd until there are 10 (12, 14) total sts.

Graft using Kitchener st.

Now it's time to add the heel! Or, if you're not yet feeling up to that, start the next sock and come back when you're feeling better.

STAR HEEL

Remove waste yarn, place live sts on needles—20 (24, 28) on each needle.

Knit 1 rnd plain.

Rnd 1: K2, SSK, k12 (20, 28), k2tog, k2; rep on 2nd needle.

Rnd 2: Knit.

Rep Rnds 1–2 until there are 10 (12, 14) sts left on each needle. Then work Rnd 1 every rnd until there are 10 (12, 14) total sts.

Graft the sts tog using Kitchener st.

FINISHING

Weave in ends.

All Sock Knitters Are Addicts

From Karida...

I learned to knit socks reluctantly. It seemed so silly to knit something with small needles that's mostly hidden by shoes. But a good friend was knitting a pair and I really wanted to wear them. So I bought some yarn and tiny needles, taught myself the magic loop technique and cast on. Now, two years later, I have knit more than a dozen pairs of sock and joined the ranks of obsessive sock knitters who loudly declare, "Sock yarn doesn't count in your stash!" Socks, I discovered, are the ultimate in portable knitting. I can fit a ball of yarn and needles for a sock in my coat pocket, and I will happily knit from it while waiting for a bus, sitting at a restaurant or hanging at the pub with my knitting friends. If you're nervous about the sock knitting bug, don't be! Go on and get bit. You'll be churning out socks in no time.

Tie-One-On Scarf

By Lindsay Henricks

Here's a quick and easy pattern for those single skeins in your stash. Using a stitch pattern that produces different textures on each side and carefully placed buttonholes, you can knit a completely reversible neck warmer. This pattern works especially well for hand-dyed yarn because it breaks up any weird pooling that might occur. Sew on matching ribbons or knit some I-cord ties to finish it off, and *voilà*! Two scarves in one!

FINISHED MEASUREMENTS
5" wide × 22½" long (13cm × 57cm)

YARN
I-CORD TIES VERSION
1 skein Cascade Venezia (merino/silk blend, 102 yds [93m] per 100g skein)
►►► *color* #126 GREEN

RIBBON TIES VERSION
1 skein Storm Moon Knits Celestial Worsted (merino, 120 yds [110m] per 100g skein)
►►► *color* PRETTY IN PINK

NEEDLES
size US 11 (8mm) straight needles
1 set of 2 size US 11 (8mm) DPNs (for I-cord ties version only)

NOTIONS
1 yd (1m) ⅞" (2cm) wide ribbon (for ribbon ties version only)
matching thread (for ribbon ties version only)
sewing needle (for ribbon ties version only)
yarn needle

GAUGE
16 sts and 20 rows = 4" (10cm) in linen st

LINEN STITCH

Row 1: *K1, sl 1 wyif; rep from * to end of row.

Row 2: *P1, sl 1 wyib; rep from * to end of row.
Rep Rows 1–2.

NECK WARMER (BOTH VERSIONS)

CO 20 sts. Work in linen st patt for 4" (10cm), ending with a WS row.

BUTTONHOLES

Row 1 (RS): K1, sl 1 wyif, k1, BO 3 sts (in patt), *sl 1 wyif, k1; rep from * to last st, sl 1 wyif.

Row 2: *P1, sl 1 wyib; rep from * to 2 sts before BO, p2, CO 3 over bound-off sts, sl 1 wyib, p1, sl 1 wyib.

Row 3: K1, sl 1 wyif, k1, [sl 1 wyif, k1 tbl] twice, *sl 1 wyif, k1; rep from * to last st, sl 1 wyif.

Row 4: *P1, sl 1 wyib; rep from * to end of row.

Row 5: *K1, sl 1 wyif; rep from * to end of row.

Row 6: *P1, sl 1 wyib; rep from * to end of row.

Rep Rows 1–3 once more to complete the buttonholes.

Work even in linen st for 15" (38cm) more, beg and ending with a WS row.

Rep buttonholes section once more.

Knit 1" (3cm) more in linen st. BO.

FINISHING

Weave in ends and block lightly. Finish neck warmer by either making I-cord ties or sewing on ribbon ties as foll:

I-CORD TIES

Using DPNs, pick up and knit 3 sts along bound-off edge of first buttonhole. Work in I-cord for 15" (38cm). Break yarn. Thread tail through rem sts, fasten off. Rep on cast-on edge of second buttonhole.

RIBBON TIES

Cut 2 15" (38cm) pieces of ribbon. Using matching thread, sew 1 ribbon to the bound-off edge of the first buttonhole. Sew the other ribbon to the cast-on edge of the second buttonhole.

To fasten, thread I-cord or ribbon ties through corresponding buttonholes at opposite end of neck warmer and tie.

Barfly Pullover

By Kate Chiocchio

Barfly is a simple pullover knit from the top down in a nice, soft superwash wool yarn, so you can spill beer on it and wash it in the machine. It is knit in one piece in the round from the top down with a simple, square neckline to eliminate any fiddly sewing. In fact, as long as you use stitch markers, you can carry on a conversation while doing the raglan increases. Waist and sleeve shaping are created with mistake-stitch ribbing for a sophisticated look that takes very little effort. Wear this sweater with jeans or over a flippy skirt with cute shoes—either way, it's flattering and comfortable.

SIZES
Women's XS (S, M, L, XL, XXL)

FINISHED MEASUREMENTS
Bust: 30 (34, 38, 42, 46, 50)" (76 [86, 97, 107, 117, 127]cm)
Length: 21 (22, 23, 24, 25, 26)" (53 [56, 58, 61, 64, 66]cm)

YARN
11 (12, 13, 15, 16, 17) skeins Mission Falls 1824 Wool Tricolors (wool, 85 yds [78m] per 50g skein)
▶▶▶ *color* #662 WILDFLOWER

NEEDLES
24" (61cm) size US 8 (5mm) circular needle (may need a longer needle for larger sizes)
1 set of 5 size US 8 (5mm) DPNs

NOTIONS
waste yarn for holders
stitch markers
yarn needle

GAUGE
20 sts and 26 rows = 4" (10cm) in St st

MISTAKE-STITCH RIB

Work over a multiple of 4 sts.

Rnd 1: *K2, p2; rep from * around.

Rnd 2: K1, *p2, k2; rep from * around to last st, k1.

Rep Rnds 1–2 for patt.

SEED STITCH

Work over a multiple of 2 sts.

Rnd 1: *K1, p1; rep from * around.

Rnd 2: *P1, k1; rep from * around.

Rep Rnds 1–2 for patt.

Notes:
Pullover is worked in 1 piece from the top down. Use lifted increases (knit into the right leg of the st in the row below, then into the st on the needle) throughout.

BODY

CO 1 st, pm, CO 8 (9, 10, 11, 12, 13) sts, pm, CO 22 (24, 30, 33, 36, 39) sts, pm, CO 8 (9, 10, 11, 12, 13) sts, pm, CO 1 st—42 (47, 52, 57, 62, 67) sts. Do not join.

Row 1 and all other WS rows: Purl, sl markers as you come to them.

Row 2: K1, inc, sl marker, inc, knit to last st before marker, inc, sl marker, inc, knit to last st before marker, inc, sl marker, inc, knit to last st before marker, inc, sl marker, inc, knit to end.

Rep Rows 1–2 a total of 4 times, then cont to work Rows 1–2 while beg to add an additional inc at each neck edge every 6 rows 4 times.

When piece measures approx 6" (15cm) or desired neck depth, CO 17 (20, 25, 28, 30, 32) sts to form the lower edge of the neck opening and join in a rnd.

Cont to work in the rnd in St st and inc at markers every other rnd as before a total of 22 (26, 27, 30, 33, 36) times, including previous inc rows—241 (280, 307, 333, 364, 395) sts.

Work even until piece measures 9½ (10, 10½, 10½, 11, 11)" (24 [25, 27, 27, 28, 28]cm) from beg.

Place 56 (61, 67, 73, 78, 83) sleeve sts from each side on waste yarn, and cont with the body as foll:

Knit to first armhole, CO 8 (8, 10, 10, 12, 12) sts, knit across to next armhole, CO 8 (8, 10, 10, 12, 12) sts, complete rnd—153 (174, 193, 211, 232, 249) sts.

Work even on body sts for 4½ (5, 5½, 6½, 7, 8)" (11 [13, 14, 17, 18, 20]cm) or desired bust length.

Next Rnd: Dec 1 (2, 1, 3, 0, 1) st(s) evenly spaced around—152 (172, 192, 208, 232, 248) sts.

Work even for 7" (18cm) in mistake-st rib. BO in patt.

SLEEVES (MAKE 2)

Place sleeve sts on DPNs. Beg at armhole, join yarn, pm, pick up and knit 8 (8, 10, 10, 12, 12) sts from CO sts for underarms. Complete rnd—60 (69, 77, 81, 90, 97) sts.

Next Rnd: Dec 0 (1, 1, 1, 0, 1) st(s)—60 (68, 76, 80, 90, 96) sts.

Working in St st, dec 1 st each side of marker every 4 (3, 3, 3, 2, 2) rnds 10 (12, 16, 16, 19, 22) times—40 (44, 44, 48, 52, 52) sts.

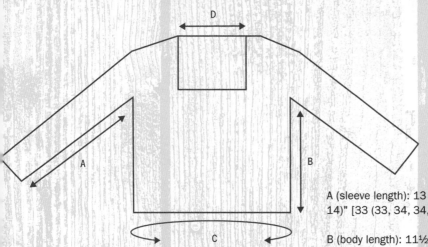

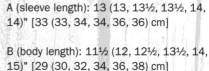

A (sleeve length): 13 (13, 13½, 13½, 14, 14)" [33 (33, 34, 34, 36, 36) cm]

B (body length): 11½ (12, 12½, 13½, 14, 15)" [29 (30, 32, 34, 36, 38) cm]

C: 30 (34, 38, 42, 46, 50)" [76 (86. 97, 107, 117, 127) cm]

D: 5 (5½, 6, 6½, 7, 7½)" [14 (14, 15, 17, 18, 19) cm]

Work even in St st until sleeve measures 7 (7, 7½, 7½, 8, 8)" (18 [18, 19, 19, 20, 20]cm) from beg.

Change to mistake-st rib and work for 6" (15cm) more. BO in patt.

FINISHING

NECKBAND

With RS facing and DPNs, start at left back shoulder seam and pick up and knit 22 (24, 30, 33, 36, 39) sts across back neck, 8 (9, 10, 11, 12, 13) sts across shoulder, 72 (74, 76, 77, 78, 79) sts around front neck, pm at lower corners, and 8 (9, 10, 11, 12, 13) sts across opposite shoulder—110 (116, 126, 132, 138, 144) sts.

Join in a rnd. Work in seed st, dec 1 st each side of markers every other rnd for 1" (3cm).

BO in patt.

Weave in ends. Block if desired.

Ruff Neck Warmer

By Karida Collins

Ruff is one of those great projects intended to look much more complicated than it actually is. Inspired by the extravagant neckwear of Elizabethan times and my general love of ruffles, this simple scarf is knit horizontally with an enlarged buttonhole that forms the "keyhole" to keep it snugly wrapped around your neck. The subtly wavy edges are made using an easy technique called ruching. Worked in simple, one-by-one ribbing and Stockinette stitch, the finished scarf is simple and whimsical with a touch of elegance.

FINISHED MEASUREMENTS
7" wide × 36" long (18cm × 91cm)

YARN
2 skeins Cascade Indulgence (superfine alpaca/angora blend, 123 yds [112m] per 50g skein)
►►► *color* #517 PURPLE

NEEDLES
32" (81cm) size US 6 (4mm) circular needle

NOTIONS
yarn needle

GAUGE
22 sts and 28 rows = 4" (10cm) in St st

SCARF

CO 200 sts. Do not join, work back and forth in rows.

Work in St st for 3" (8cm), ending with a WS row.

CENTER DECREASE

Next Row (RS): *P2tog; rep from * across—100 sts.

Next Row: *K1, p1; rep from * across.

Work even in rib until piece measures 3½" (9cm) from beg, ending with a WS row.

KEYHOLE OPENING

Row 1 (RS): *K1, p1; rep from * until 18 sts rem, BO next 16 sts, cont in rib to end of row.

Row 2: *K1, p1; rep from * to bound-off sts.

CO 16 sts over bound-off sts using backward-loop method, cont in rib to end of row.

Work even in rib until piece measures 4" (10cm) from beg, ending with a WS row.

Next Row (RS): *Kfb; rep from * across—200 sts.

Work in St st until piece measures 7" (18cm) from beg.

BO loosely.

FINISHING

Weave in ends.

Theme Movie Night

From Karida...

Another good knitter's night in is a movie night. Pick a movie (or movies) and plan your projects accordingly. Challenge yourself to match the drinking to the movie, too. Knit Victorian-style lace while watching *Jane Eyre* and sipping cordials. Drink scotch, work on a cabled aran sweater and watch *Braveheart*. Or just invite a few friends over to watch your favorite movies, drink your favorite drinks and knit your favorite projects. My favorite combination is white wine and the *Buffy the Vampire Slayer* series on DVD. Whenever I'm trying to finish a pile of gifts at the holidays, I invite knitting friends in the same situation over for a marathon of knitting, Buffy and booze.

Fizzy Sweater

By Libby Bruce

This little number is named for the eyelets incorporated into the rib, which remind me of champagne bubbles. *Fizzy* is an allover rib sweater worked from the bottom up. The square neckline, fitted shoulder and elbow-length sleeves are inspired by the romantic period dresses worn by Jane Austen's heroines. The deep, stretchy puff rib pattern requires no shaping. Eye-catching and edgy, yet traditional and elegant, *Fizzy* is both a fun knit and a welcome addition to your winter wardrobe.

SIZES
Women's XS (S, M, L, XL, XXL)

FINISHED MEASUREMENTS
Bust: 30 (33, 36, 39, 42, 45)" (76 [84, 91, 99, 107, 114]cm)
Length: 22 (22½, 23, 24½, 25, 25)" (56 [57, 58, 62, 64, 64]cm)

Note: Puff rib fabric is super stretchy. It is very easy to resize this sweater—just add or subtract multiples of 3 sts to the body. Be careful, though—it's stretchier than it looks! It can be worn with up to 2" to 3" (5cm to 8cm) of negative ease.

YARN
8 (8, 9, 9, 10, 11) skeins Cascade Cash Vero (merino/microfiber/cashmere blend, 98 yds [90m] per 50g skein)
▶▶▶ *color #028 BLUE*

NEEDLES
24" (61cm) size US 7 (4.5mm) circular needle
1 set of 5 size US 7 (4.5mm) DPNs

NOTIONS
stitch markers
split ring markers
yarn needle

GAUGE
14 sts and 22 rows = 4" (10cm) in patt st
16 sts and 22 rows = 4" (10 cm) in St st

BODY

CO 105 (114, 126, 135, 147, 156) sts. Pm and join, being careful not to twist.

Work in puff rib patt as foll:

Rnd 1: *P2, yo, k1, yo; rep from * around.

Rnds 2–3: (P2, k3) around.

Rnd 4: (P2, k3tog) around.

Rep Rnds 1–4 until piece measures 16 (16, 16, 17, 17, 17)" (41 [41, 41, 43, 43, 43]cm) from beg, ending with Rnd 4.

SHAPE SHOULDERS

Note: In this section you will use split ring markers to mark your knitting. In this case, the markers go on the actual st, not on the needle.

Next Row (RS): BO 9 sts, k9, BO 25 (30, 36, 40, 46, 51) sts, k9, BO 9 sts, pm, BO 9 sts, pm, BO 26 (30, 36, 41, 47, 51) sts, pm, BO 9 sts, pm.

Working separately, work the 2 9-st wide straps in St st until they measure 12 (13, 14, 15, 16, 16)" (30 [33, 36, 38, 41, 41]cm). BO.

Position bound-off edge of strap between split ring markers on back of piece. Seam. Remove markers.

SLEEVES (MAKE 2)

Starting at front outside edge of shoulder cap, pick up and knit 42 (46, 50, 54, 58, 62) sts around armhole opening.

Pm and join in a rnd. Work in St st until sleeve measures 12" (30cm) or desired length.

Work in garter st (k1 row, p1 row) for 1" (3cm). BO.

FINISHING

Weave in ends, close gaps under arms (if any).

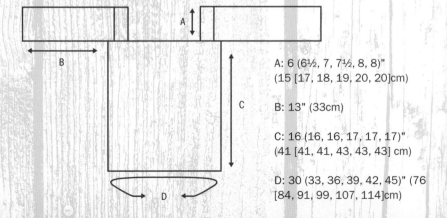

A: 6 (6½, 7, 7½, 8, 8)" (15 [17, 18, 19, 20, 20]cm)

B: 13" (33cm)

C: 16 (16, 16, 17, 17, 17)" (41 [41, 41, 43, 43, 43] cm)

D: 30 (33, 36, 39, 42, 45)" (76 [84, 91, 99, 107, 114]cm)

No Stain, No Pain

From Libby...

If you're worried about spills, be sure to check out the tips on page 119 for removing stains. Or try these stain-free drinks.

1. *Vodka tonic* (just ask the *Hangover Lap Blanket* [see page 138]. It once drank half a vodka tonic, and it ended up being famous in a book!)

2. *White wine*

3. *Gin and tonic*

4. *Martini*

5. *Mojito*

Absinthe Sweater

By Jessica Kleinmann & Libby Bruce

Fibre Company Terra is a beautiful, special yarn. And this sweater is a perfect vehicle for it: Simple and unique, it maximizes the yardage of these pretty skeins so you get the most bang for your luxury-fiber buck. The overlapping collar, boatneck shape and tubular cast on add interest to an otherwise simple sweater.

SIZES
Women's XS (S, M, L, XL, XXL)

FINISHED MEASUREMENTS
Bust: 30 (33, 36, 39, 42, 45)" (76 [84, 91, 99, 107, 114]cm)
Length: 17 (18, 19, 20, 21, 22)" (43 [46, 48, 51, 53, 56]cm)

YARN
8 (8, 9, 10, 11, 12) skeins Fibre Company Terra (merino/baby alpaca/silk blend, 100 yds [91m] per 50g skein)
►►► *color* BLUE SPRUCE

NEEDLES
size US 7 (4.5mm) straight needles

NOTIONS
waste yarn
stitch markers
yarn needle

GAUGE
18 sts and 28 rows = 4" (10cm) in St st

SSK (slip, slip, knit): Dec 1 st by slipping 2 sts knitwise 1 at a time, inserting the tip of the left needle into both sts and knitting the 2 sts tog.

M1 (make 1): Inc 1 st by picking up the bar between the next st and the st just knit and knitting into it.

K2tog (knit 2 together): Dec 1 st by knitting 2 sts tog.

Pm (place marker): Slip a premade marker or a loosely knotted piece of scrap yarn in a contrasting color onto the right needle after the st just knit to mark a spot in the knitting to refer to on future rows. When you come to a marker, simply slip it from the right-hand needle to the left-hand needle.

BODY (MAKE 2)

Using a tubular method, CO 68 (74, 80, 88, 94, 102) sts.

Work in k1, p1 ribbing for 2" (5cm).

Work in St st for ½" (1cm), ending with a RS row.

SHAPE WAIST

Next Row (WS): P23, pm, p22 (28, 34, 42, 48, 56), pm, p23.

Next (Dec) Row (RS): Knit to marker, sl marker, k2tog; knit to 2 sts before 2nd marker, SSK, knit to end.

Rep Dec Row every 6th row twice more—62 (68, 74, 82, 88, 96) sts.

Work even in St st for 2" (5cm), ending with a WS row.

Next (Inc) Row (RS): Knit to marker, sl marker, M1; knit to 1 st before 2nd marker, M1, knit to end.

Rep Inc Row every 6th row twice more—68 (74, 80, 88, 94, 102) sts.

Work even in St st until piece measures 10 (10½, 11, 11½, 12, 12½)" (25 [27, 28, 29, 30, 32]cm) from beg, ending with a WS row.

Tubular Cast On

This is a funny little cast on that makes a nice, pretty edge and is also good for things that need an elastic hem, such as socks.

1. With waste yarn, cast on half the number of stitches required.

2. Switch to your main yarn.

3. Purl one row, knit one row.

4. Repeat step 3.

5. You're now at the beginning of a Wrong Side row. Purl the first stitch. Easy enough.

6. Now, look down to your waste yarn row. See the backside of the very first stitch you knitted in your main yarn? It'll be a little different-colored bar.

7. Using your left needle, pick up that stitch. Then knit it.

8. Purl one stitch.

9. Reach down and grab the second stitch you knitted in your main yarn. Knit it.

10. Repeat steps 8 and 9 until you get to the end. You'll purl your last stitch, and you'll see a little wonky knot on the very end of the tube. That's your last stitch to pick up. Don't sweat the wonkyness, just pick it up and knit it. Pull out the waste yarn. Done!

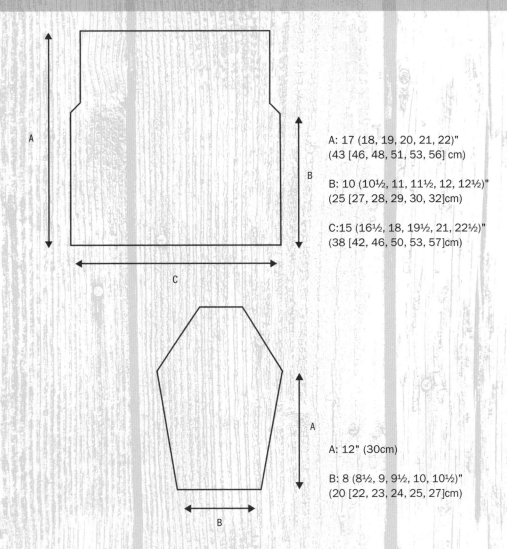

A: 17 (18, 19, 20, 21, 22)"
(43 [46, 48, 51, 53, 56] cm)

B: 10 (10½, 11, 11½, 12, 12½)"
(25 [27, 28, 29, 30, 32]cm)

C:15 (16½, 18, 19½, 21, 22½)"
(38 [42, 46, 50, 53, 57]cm)

A: 12" (30cm)

B: 8 (8½, 9, 9½, 10, 10½)"
(20 [22, 23, 24, 25, 27]cm)

SHAPE ARMHOLES

Next (Dec) Row (RS): K1, SSK, knit to last 3 sts, k2tog, k1.

Rep Dec Row every RS row 5 (5, 6, 6, 7, 7) times more—56 (62, 66, 74, 78, 86) sts.

Work even in St st until piece measures 15 (16, 17, 18, 19, 20)" (38 [41, 43, 46, 48, 51]cm), ending with a WS row.

SHAPE NECK

Next Row (RS): K20 (23, 25, 28, 30, 33), join 2nd ball of yarn and BO center 16 (16, 16, 18, 18, 20) sts, k20 (23, 25, 28, 30, 33).

Working both sides at once, BO 5 sts at each neck edge twice—10 (13, 15, 18, 20, 23) sts rem on each side.

BO 3 (3, 4, 5, 5, 5) sts at each neck edge 3 times—1 (4, 3, 3, 5, 8) sts rem on each side.

Work even until piece measures 17 (18, 19, 20, 21, 22)" (43 [46, 48, 51, 53, 56]cm). BO.

SLEEVES (MAKE 2)

Using a tubular method, CO 36 (38, 40, 42, 46, 48) sts. Work in k1, p1 ribbing for 2" (5cm).

Work in St st for 1" (3cm), ending with a WS row.

Next (Inc) Row (RS): M1 at beg and end of every 6th row 8 (8, 9, 9, 10, 10) times—52 (54, 58, 60, 66, 68) sts.

Work even in St st until sleeve measures 12" (30cm), ending with a WS row.

SHAPE CAP

Next (Dec) Row (RS): K1, SSK, knit to last 3 sts, k2tog, k1.

Rep Dec Row every RS row 6 times—40 (42, 46, 48, 54, 56) sts.

Cont to work Dec Row every RS row until 22 sts rem.

BO 2 sts at beg of next 6 rows—10 sts.

BO all sts.

FINISHING

Fit in sleeves and seam, sew side and sleeve seams. Do not seam at shoulders.

COLLAR

Pick up and knit 56 (62, 66, 74, 78, 86) sts across front edge. Work in k1, p1 ribbing for 2" (5cm). BO using tubular method.

Rep for back.

Fold collar edges over one another at the sides and seam in place to form shoulder caps.

Weave in ends. Block if desired.

Tubular Bind Off in K1, P1 Rib

I am not going to lie to you. This bind off is seriously finicky. It's not hard, it just takes some practice. I'm not saying don't bother with it—I just want you to know what you're in for.

1. Finish your last row and leave all stitches on the needle. Cut the working yarn, leaving an extra long tail. Seriously long. You don't want to run out.

2. Thread a yarn needle with the tail.

3. Stick the needle into the first stitch (a knit stitch) as if to knit.

4. Pull the yarn through the stitch, tighten 'til it's snug, then drop the stitch off the needle.

5. Skip over that purl stitch and stick your yarn needle purlwise into the second stitch on the needle—this will be a knit stitch, too.

6. Pull the yarn all the way though.

7. Stick the yarn needle purlwise into that abandoned purl stitch you skipped over before.

8. Pull it 'til it's snug and drop it. The knit stitch you threaded through before is still on the knitting needle.

9. Take your yarn needle behind the knitting and stick it through in between the first and second stitches on the needle. (You're not picking up any stitches or anything here, you're just going straight under the needle, above the knitting.) Pull the yarn through.

10. Stick the needle into the second stitch (the purl stitch) knitwise. Pull the yarn through. Don't drop anything.

11. Repeat steps 3 through 10 until you've bound off all the stitches. Have a glass of wine.

One WIP is Never Enough

From Both of Us...

It is good practice to always have at least two projects on the needles. (We usually roll with about eight or nine in various stages of completion...but this isn't about us.) The real key is to make sure you always have something easy rolling. That way, you'll always have something relaxing to knit and a good project for social knitting to boot.

We call any knitting project-in-progress a WIP (short for work-in-progress, obviously).

Karida's WIPs

- more dishrags to match the red and pink in the kitchen
- Airy Wraparound Lace Sweater by Stefanie Japel from *Fitted Knits*
- Modernist Stripe Sleep Sacque by Mary-Heather Cougar
- cabled dog sweaters for Honey and Trixie, my rat terriers (tiny dogs = portable sweaters!)
- Pi shawl by Elizabeth Zimmerman
- Knitted Garter Stitch Blanket by Elizabeth Zimmerman (perfect knitting for movie watching with a glass of wine)
- *Dancing Bamboo Socks* (see page 28) for me
- *K.I.S.S. Leg Warmers* (see page 128) in worsted weight yarn
- Textured Circle Shrug by Stefanie Japel from *Glam Knits*

Libby's WIPs

- *Woozy Washrag* (see page 110) in red and white (to match my kitchen)
- bulky green cabled sweater
- Alexandra Ballet Top by Stefanie Japel from *Fitted Knits*
- Fair Isle hat and scarf set for Mom
- Hedera socks by Cookie A.
- Barbara Walker sampler blanket in 12 colors of Mission Falls 1824 wool (I plan to work on this 'til I'm 80)
- another *Fizzy Sweater* (see page 66). (You can't have too many—this one's orange)

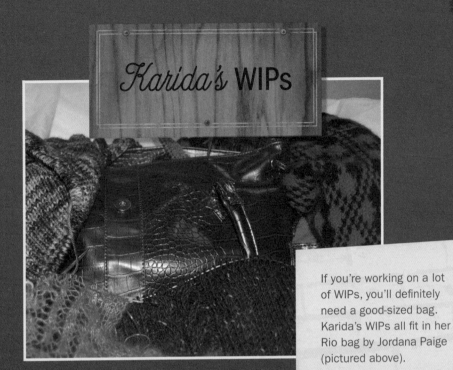

Karida's WIPs

If you're working on a lot of WIPs, you'll definitely need a good-sized bag. Karida's WIPs all fit in her Rio bag by Jordana Paige (pictured above).

Libby's WIPs

Don't Forget Your Mittens!

By Karida Collins

Have you ever left the bar (or shop or restaurant) on a wintry night and realized once you stepped into the cold that you forgot your mittens? Or maybe you didn't even realize you left them until you got home! Now you don't have to worry about leaving precious handknits. This scarf/mitten combo updates the idea of a child's mittens connected by a string into the perfect winter accessory for a forgetful adult. Even if you never forget anything, you'll love the simplicity and versatility of this easy scarf with mittens attached. Best of all, the pattern is customizable for any length of arms so you won't ever end up with a scarf that is too short or too long.

SIZES
Customizable

FINISHED MEASUREMENTS
5" wide × 90" long (13cm × 229cm), excluding mittens, or size to fit

YARN
4 skeins Shibui Knits Merino Alpaca (baby alpaca/merino wool blend, 131 yds [120m] per 100g skein)
▶▶▶ *color* #229 MULBERRY (A)
2 skeins Shibui Knits Merino Alpaca
▶▶▶ *color* #220 PEONY (B)

NEEDLES
size US 9 (5.5mm) straight needles
1 set of 5 size US 7 (4.5mm) DPNs

NOTIONS
stitch markers
waste yarn
yarn needle

GAUGE
16 sts and 20 rows = 4" (10cm) in k2, p2 ribbing using larger needles

3

CALCULATE LENGTH

With arms outstretched at sides, have a friend measure you from wrist to wrist across the back. This number is X. Multiply X by 1.5. This product will be the length of your scarf (without the mittens). Since you'll be knitting the scarf one half at a time, divide X by 2. This number is Y—the length of each scarf half. Don't skip the measuring! If your scarf is a gift and you can't measure, estimate the person's height and use that number as X. The sample was knit for a 5'7" (8m) woman with an X number of 60" (152cm); therefore, the sample is 90" (229cm), excluding the mittens. The scarf should be long enough to wrap around the neck at least once and reach the hands without pulling tightly.

RIGHT SCARF HALF

With larger needles and A, provisionally CO 40 sts using your preferred method.

Note: There are an infinite number of cast-on methods. My favorite (the invisible loop provisional CO) is explained thoroughly by Amy on her Web site, KnittingHelp.com.

Work in k2, p2 ribbing for Y" (Y times 2.54cm), ending with a WS row.

Do not BO. Begin working mitten.

RIGHT MITTEN

Transfer 40 sts to DPNs (smaller needles). The open sides of the scarf are on the side of hand opposite the thumb. This marks the beg of rnd.

With smaller needles and B, work in k2, p2 ribbing across all sts. Pm and join in a rnd.

CUFF

Cont in k2, p2 ribbing for 2½" (6cm).

Change to St st and work even for 6 rnds.

THUMB GUSSET

Rnd 1: K18, pm, M1, k4, M1, pm, knit to end.

Rnd 2: Knit.

Rep these 2 rnds 4 more times—50 sts, 10 sts between gusset markers.

Next Rnd: Knit to first marker. Sl next 10 sts onto waste yarn. Using backward-loop method, CO 4 sts over gap. Knit rest of rnd—44 sts for hand.

Work even in St st until St st portion measures 5" (13cm) or 1" (3cm) below tip of tallest finger.

TOP DECREASES

Distribute sts evenly over 4 needles.

Rnd 1: Needles 1 and 3: K1, k2tog, knit across needle.

Rnd 1: Needles 2 and 4: Knit to last 3 sts, SSK, k1.

Rnd 2: All needles: Knit.

Rep these 2 rnds twice more—32 sts.

Rep Rnd 1–4 times more—16 sts.

Distribute rem sts on 2 needles. Break yarn, leaving a long tail for grafting. Use Kitchener st to graft sts tog, closing mitten top.

THUMB

Place 10 gusset sts on 2 needles. Use third needle to pick up and knit 5 sts at base of thumb at gap—15 sts.

Pm and join in a rnd.

Work even in St st for 1" (3cm).

Rnd 1: *K1, k2tog; rep from * around—10 sts.

Rnd 2: K1, *k2tog, k1; rep from * around—7 sts.

Break yarn. Thread tail through rem 7 sts, fasten off.

LEFT SCARF HALF AND MITTEN

Complete as for right half, except last row of scarf should be a RS row. Open sides of scarf should be on outside of hand, opposite thumb, and mark beg of rnd.

FINISHING

Carefully remove provisional cast on yarn and sl provisional sts to larger needle on each side, making certain thumbs are oriented properly.

Using A and yarn needle, graft 2 halves tog with Kitchener st.

Weave in ends and lightly block.

Raspberry Wheat Ale Messenger Bag

By Kate Chiocchio

This bag is meant to be a simple project you can knit anywhere. You don't need to pay close attention, and if you are involved in a conversation and knit a few too many rows, don't worry. Just make sure you knit the front and back about thirty percent higher than you want the finished bag to be and ten to twenty percent wider. It is meant to be roomy and can easily carry an entire sweater project.

SIZES
Customizable

FINISHED MEASUREMENTS
14" high × 19" long × 4" deep (36cm × 48cm × 10cm), before felting
9½" high × 17" long × 3½" deep (24cm × 43cm × 9cm), after felting

YARN
5 skeins Cascade 220 (wool, 220 yds [201m] per 100g skein)
►►► *color* #9488 RED

NEEDLES
size US 10 (6mm) straight needles

NOTIONS
1 yd (1m) ¾" (2cm) ribbon in coordinating color
embroidery floss in coordinating color
sewing needle and coordinating thread
yarn needle

GAUGE
20 sts and 28 rows = 4" (10cm) in St st before felting

NOTES

YO (yarn over): Wrap the working yarn around the needle clockwise, and knit the next st as usual. This operation creates an eyelet hole in the knitting and inc 1 st.

K2tog (knit 2 together): Dec 1 st by knitting 2 sts tog.

FRONT

CO 95 sts. Knit in St st for 14" (36cm). BO.

BACK AND FLAP

CO 95 sts. Knit in St st for 29" (74cm).

Knit 8 rows in garter st. BO.

GUSSET

CO 20 sts. Knit in garter st for 47" (119cm). BO.

RIBBED POCKETS (MAKE 2)

CO 20 sts. Work in k2, p2 ribbing to 8" (20cm) or desired length. BO. Do not full (this pocket will remain unfelted).

FELTED POCKET

CO 70 sts. Knit in St st for 11" (28cm), ending with a WS row.

Next (Eyelet) Row (RS): K2tog, *yo, k2tog; rep from * to end of row.

Next Row: Purl.

Knit 6 more rows in St st. BO.

STRAP

CO 13 sts.

Next Row: K9, move yarn to front, sl 4 sts purlwise.

Rep last row until strap measures 38" (97cm) or desired length. BO.

FINISHING

Whipstitch front and back to gusset. Sew ends of strap to top edges of gusset. Weave in ends.

FELTING

Now, for the fun part! Weave in your ends, but don't cut them. Place your big, floppy bag and large pocket in a mesh laundry bag (the kind with zippers works best). Wash it in hot water with a moderate amount of soap. I use the regular cycle and throw in a pair of jeans for added agitation. (Remember to check the jeans pockets first—tissues left in your pockets can cause you to spend hours picking little white lint out of your beautiful new bag.) Check your bag frequently and when it is the size and fabric you like, spin out the water, shape it and let it dry. To help achieve the size and shape you want, stuff the bag with wadded-up newspapers, books, old videotapes or soda bottles. Don't be afraid to stretch your bag to the dimensions you want. See Get Felt Up, page 86, for more information on felting.

Once the bag has dried, cut off all your yarn tails. Sew ribbed pockets inside the side panels using whipstitch and leftover yarn. Cut ribbon in half and sew each end to the WS of the pocket at each end with a sewing needle. Thread the ribbon through the top of the bag and tie it in a pretty bow. Using a tapestry needle and embroidery floss, whipstitch the pocket to the inside back of the bag, being careful not to push the needle all the way though to the other side of the fabric. Because the fulled fabric is so heavy, sts will not show on outside of piece.

Get Felt Up

From Libby...

Easy, fun, stylish, functional: Felt is ideal for the social knitter.

Patterns for felting, by nature, don't include fancy stitchwork. Felted projects are often small and portable, and (the best part) if you screw up, it probably won't matter. I am not saying you can destroy the pattern into bits and still get what you're hoping for at the end. What I mean is, tension doesn't really matter. Funky looking stitches don't matter. You can miss an increase or a decrease, and that probably won't matter either. This makes it ideal, simply ideal, for knittin' and drankin'.

But I Ain't Never Felted Before!

Baby, it's easy. I suspect you or someone you know has done it by accident before. Here are the main things you need to know.

Make sure you start with the right yarn. Not all yarn will felt. It has to be 100% (or close to 100%) animal fiber, like wool or alpaca. It can't be machine washable! And it can't be bright white. (All that bleach makes the wool grumpy and noncompliant.)

If you're not sure if something will felt, ask the nice lady or gentleman at the yarn store. They'll know.

OK, I Knitted a Giant Misshapen Thing. What Now?

Put it in the washer. If you've got a front-loading machine, good for you for conserving water! But you might want to borrow a friend's top loader for this part. You can felt in a front loader, but since you can't open it in the middle of a cycle, you have less control over the size.

It's a good idea to stick it in a zippered pillowcase first. You can also throw in an old pair of jeans or an old towel. (This will give the garment something to mingle with and speed up the felting.) Put in a little detergent, and set the washer to hot. Check on your garment every now and then to make sure things are on track. Depending on the yarn you chose and your washer, this could take more than one cycle.

Here's the tricky part: Do not let it over-felt. There is no way to unfelt something. If it shrinks too much, you're stuck with it.

When it's the right size, take it out and squeeze out the extra water. Shape your garment (either by laying it flat or by stuffing it with plastic grocery bags) and let it air-dry.

Told you it was easy.

Here is a fishy wine cozy before felting. Note how the top edge is curling and the Fair Isle colorwork looks a little wonky.

And now look! Here he is all felted up. The top has straightened out, and the fishies look much clearer. Even the bottom is all nice and even.

Sideways Scarf

By Libby Bruce

Horizontal scarves are always a little surprising to the eye. With its alternating stitch patterns that sometimes change in the middle of a row, this scarf is surprising in more ways than one. It is the kind of knitting that a couple of glasses of wine might produce—sideways, with uneven stripes and seemingly random stitch patterns. It has the added bonus of allowing any mistakes to look intentional. Portable, easy and designed to camouflage mistakes, this scarf is perfect pub knitting!

NOTES

pm (place marker): Slip a premade marker or a loosely knotted piece of scrap yarn in a contrasting color onto the right needle after the st just knit to mark a spot in the knitting to refer to on future rows. When you come to a marker, simply slip it from the right-hand needle to the left-hand needle.

SCARF

CO 240 sts, pm at 120 sts (center).

Rows 1–4: With A, knit.

Row 5: With B, purl.

Row 6: With B, knit.

Row 7: With B, purl.

Row 8: With B, knit to marker, purl to end.

Rows 9–10: With C, knit to marker, purl to end.

Rows 11–14: With C, knit.

Row 15: With A, purl.

Rows 16–18: With A, purl to marker, knit to end.

Rows 18–21: With D, knit.

Rep Rows 1–21 once more. Bind off.

FINISHING

Weave in ends.

FINISHED MEASUREMENTS

6" wide × 60" long (15cm × 152cm)

YARN

2 skeins Karabella Aurora 8 (100% wool, 98 yds [90m] per 50g skein) in each of the foll colors:
▶▶▶ *color* #910 PURPLE (A)
▶▶▶ *color* #716 PARSLEY (B)
1 skein Karabella Aurora 8 in each of the foll colors:
▶▶▶ *color* #190 BLUE (C)
▶▶▶ *color* #49 BROWN (D)

NEEDLES

40" (102cm) size US 7 (4.5mm) circular needle

NOTIONS

stitch marker
yarn needle

GAUGE

16 sts = 4" (10cm) in garter st

Slouchy Hat

By Karida Collins

Winter in Washington, DC, is not exactly arctic. But it still gets pretty cold and windy and damp. So you need a nice sturdy hat. Now I have a lot of hair. Think 1970s 'fro. Regular knit hat styles just don't do much for me and all my hair. Enter the *Slouchy Hat*. Easy Stockinette stitch in the round combined with beret styling and super bulky yarn make for a quick knit with dramatic results. Guaranteed to contain the largest of hairstyles.

FINISHED MEASUREMENTS
24" (61cm) head circumference

YARN
2 skeins Neighborhood Fiber Co. Victorian Bulky (wool, 64 yds [59m] per 114g skein)
▶▶▶ *color* SHERIDAN CIRCLE

NEEDLES
16" (41cm) size US 15 (10mm) circular needle

NOTIONS
stitch marker
yarn needle

GAUGE
6 sts and 10 rows = 4" (10cm) in St st

NOTES

M1 (make 1): Inc 1 st by picking up the bar between the next st and the st just knit and knitting into it.

K2tog (knit 2 together): Dec 1 st by knitting 2 sts tog.

BRIM

With DPNs, CO 36 sts. Pm and join, being careful not to twist. Sts should be evenly distributed on needles.

Next Rnd: *K2, p2; rep from * around. Cont in this manner until brim measures 2" (5cm) from beg.

BODY

Next Rnd: *K4, M1; rep from * around—45 sts.

Change to circular needle when needed.

Knit 2 rnds.

Next Rnd: *K5, M1; rep from * around—54 sts.

Knit 2 rnds.

Next Rnd: *K6, M1; rep from * around—63 sts.

Work even in St st until piece measures 9" (23cm) from beg.

CROWN DECREASES

Change to DPNs when needed.

Next Rnd: *K7, k2tog; rep from * around— 56 sts.

Knit 3 rnds.

Next Rnd: *K6, k2tog; rep from * around— 49 sts.

Knit 2 rnds.

Next Rnd: *K5, k2tog; rep from * around— 42 sts.

Knit 1 rnd.

Next Rnd: *K4, k2tog; rep from * around— 35 sts.

Knit 1 rnd.

Next Rnd: *K3, k2tog; rep from * around— 28 sts.

Next Rnd: *K2, k2tog; rep from * around— 21 sts.

Next Rnd: *K1, k2tog; rep from * around— 14 sts.

Next Rnd: *K2tog; rep from * around—7 sts.

Break yarn. Thread tail through rem 7 sts, fasten off.

FINISHING

Weave in ends. Block and enjoy!

Knitting with DPNs

From Karida...

I hate knitting with double-pointed needles, but they are the easiest way to finish the top of a hat. If this is your first time using DPNs, don't worry. I'll walk you through it.

► First, be sober. If you're already four drinks in and you've never made the DPN switch, put down the hat and pick up your backup project.

► Count the stitches on your circular needle and divide by four to figure out how many stitches will go on each DPN. For example, if you have forty-five stitches and a set of four DPNs, that's fifteen stitches per needle. The fifth DPN is the working needle. You don't put stitches on that one.

► Pick up the first DPN and the circular needle. Starting at the break in your knitting, slide the correct number of stitches onto the DPN. Now grab the next needle and repeat the process, continuing around the circular needle.

► Once the stitches have been evenly distributed, you're ready to keep working in the round. Grab that working needle (the one with no stitches). Use it to knit the stitches on Needle 1 (the first needle you used to move stitches). At the end of this process, all the stitches from Needle 1 should be on the working needle. Now Needle 1 is empty and becomes the new working needle.

► Repeat the process with the other needles, and you should be working in the round just fine.

► Remember, if it's the crown of a hat, you shouldn't have too many rows to work on DPNs. And it's okay if you feel like you're handling a sharp, pointy octopus. That's how I feel, too.

Two-Fisted Tank

By Karida Collins

This tank is super simple. Knit from the bottom up, it is essentially a ribbed tube. There is no shaping because the ribbing will help the garment hug your shape in all the right places. Finally, the straps and armholes at the top are formed with a creatively lopsided buttonhole. You might need to be sober to do the armhole (never underestimate the difficulty of counting), but the rest is definitely perfect bar knitting.

SIZES
Women's XS (S, M, L, XL, XXL)

FINISHED MEASUREMENTS
Bust: 30 (33, 36, 39, 42, 45)" (76 [84, 91, 99, 107, 114]cm)
Length: 20 (20, 22, 22, 24, 24)" (51 [51, 56, 56, 61, 61]cm)

Note: Knit in cotton-blend yarn, this garment demands negative ease. Choose a size approx 2" (5cm) smaller than your actual bust measurement. Seriously. You'll thank me later.

YARN
4 (4, 5, 6, 7, 8) skeins Cascade Cotton Club (cotton/acrylic blend, 98 yds [90m] per 50g skein)
►►► *color #19292 YELLOW*

NEEDLES
24" (61cm) size US 7 (4.5mm) circular needle

NOTIONS
stitch markers
yarn needle

GAUGE
16 sts and 20 rows = 4" (10cm) in k2, p2 ribbing

BODY

CO 120 (132, 144, 156, 168, 180) sts. Pm and join, being careful not to twist. Work in k2, p2 ribbing until piece measures 18 (18, 20, 20, 22, 22)" (46 [46, 51, 51, 56, 56]cm) from beg.

DIVIDE FOR ARMHOLES

Rnd 1: Remove marker. Work in patt for 116 (128, 138, 150, 160, 172) sts, pm to mark new beg of rnd.

Note: For sizes M and L, this change will result in a rnd that begins with p2 instead of k2. Adjust accordingly to maintain st patt.

Rnd 2: BO 8 (8, 12, 12, 16, 16) sts, work in patt for 52 (58, 60, 66, 68, 74) sts, BO 8 (8, 12, 12, 16, 16) sts, work in patt for 52 (58, 60, 66, 68, 74) sts.

Rnd 3: Using the backwards-loop method, CO 24 (32, 40, 48, 56, 64) sts, work in patt for 52 (58, 60, 66, 68, 74) sts, CO 24 (32, 40, 48, 56, 64) sts, work in patt for 52 (58, 60, 66, 68, 74) sts—152 (180, 200, 228, 248, 276) sts.

YOKE

Work in k2, p2 ribbing until piece measures 20 (20, 22, 22, 24, 24)" (51 [51, 56, 56, 61, 61]cm) from beg.

BO loosely. Hint: Using a larger needle to bind off will prevent a too-tight edge.

FINISHING

Weave in ends, block and enjoy!

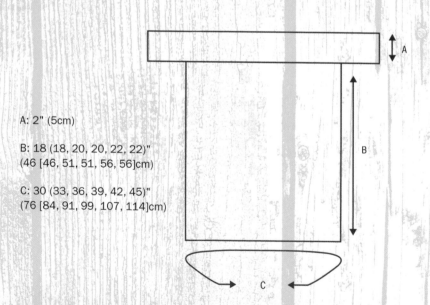

A: 2" (5cm)

B: 18 (18, 20, 20, 22, 22)"
(46 [46, 51, 51, 56, 56]cm)

C: 30 (33, 36, 39, 42, 45)"
(76 [84, 91, 99, 107, 114]cm)

College Colors Cozies

By Libby Bruce & Karida Collins

Nothing says *Pints & Purls* like a felted cozy for your booze! These little guys can be knitted up in an evening, and they are both novel and functional.

You could really get creative with these patterns. Change the colors to match your school, your Hogwarts House, your favorite beer, your kitchen, your dog's spots, your favorite outfit...the possibilities are endless. We've shown them here in Ohio State and rainbow colors.

FINISHED MEASUREMENTS

approx 9¼" (24cm) around × 3¼" (8cm) high, after felting

YARN

OHIO STATE VERSION
1 skein Cascade 220 (100% wool, 220 yds [201m] per 100g skein) in each of the foll colors:
►►► *color* #9404 SCARLET
►►► *color* #9473 GRAY

RAINBOW VERSION
1 skein Ella Rae Classic (100% wool, 219 yds [200m] per 100g skein) in each of the foll colors:
►►► *color* #30 BLUE
►►► *color* #33 ORANGE
►►► *color* #31 RED
►►► *color* #44 GOLD
►►► *color* #28 PURPLE
►►► *color* #29 GREEN

NEEDLES

size US 10 (6mm) DPNs

GAUGE

Gauge is not important

NOTES

K2tog (**knit** 2 together): Dec 1 st by knitting 2 sts tog.

COZY

CO 36 sts. Join for working in the rnd, taking care not to twist sts.

Work in k1, p1 rib for 1 rnd.

Knit for 5" (13cm), changing colors every 4 rnds.

BOTTOM

Row 1: K2tog around.

Rows 2–3: Knit.

Rows 4–5: K2tog around.

Break yarn, thread tail through rem 6 sts.

FINISHING

Weave in ends.

Felt in hot water until desired size.
(See page 86 for detailed felting instructions.)

Drink-Like-a-Fish Cozy

By Libby Bruce

Felting is a fantastic way to experiment with colorwork, since gaps and uneven stitches, the main pitfalls of multicolor knitting, tend to disappear when the piece is felted. These little Fair Isle fish are fun to knit, not to mention adorable. Stick on some googly eyes, and suddenly your beer is a conversation piece.

FINISHED MEASUREMENTS
7½" tall × 9" circumference (19cm × 23cm), after felting

YARN
1 skein Ella Rae Classic (wool, 219 yds [200m] per 100g skein) in each of the foll colors:
▶▶▶ *color* #29 GREEN (A)
▶▶▶ *color* #27 ORANGE (B)

NEEDLES
1 set of 5 size US 10 (6mm) DPNs

NOTIONS
1 hook-and-eye closure
3 ½" (1cm) sew-on wiggle eyes
sewing needle and thread
stitch marker
yarn needle

GAUGE
Gauge is not important

NECK

With B, CO 20 sts.

Row 1 (WS): Purl.

Row 2: Knit.

Row 3: With A, purl.

Row 4: K1, M1, knit to 2nd to last st, M1, k1.

Rep Rows 1–4 4 times, changing colors every 2 rows—28 sts.

Cont in St st, work 2 rows with B.

BODY

Next Row (RS): With B, CO 10 sts. Pm and join for working in the rnd—36 sts.

Cont with A, work in St st until piece measures 1½" (4cm) from join.

Cont in the rnd, work fishy chart over 12 sts 3 times. Work even in A until piece measures 6" (15cm) from join.

BOTTOM

Rnd 1: *K2tog; rep from * around—19 sts.

Rnds 2–3: Knit.

Rnd 4: K1, *k2tog; rep from * around—9 sts.

Rnd 5: K1, *k2tog; rep from * around—4 sts.

Break yarn. Thread tail through rem 4 sts, fasten off.

FINISHING

Weave in ends.

Felt in hot water until desired size. While the cozy is still wet, put it on a beer bottle and use a safety pin to pull the neck shut. Allow it to dry in this way until it holds its shape. When the cozy is dry, sew on the hook-and-eye closure at the top of the neck. Affix a wiggle eye to each fish. Drink beer with it and amaze your friends.

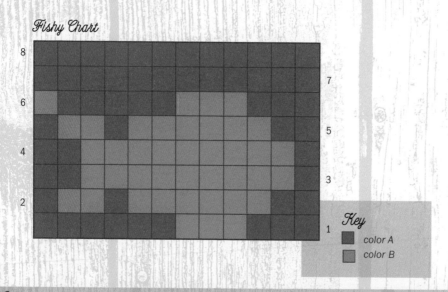

Fishy Chart

Key
■ color A
■ color B

Wine Bottle Sweater

By Karida Collins

Any good sommelier (professional wine geek) will tell you that wine should be stored in a dark place. But maybe you keep your wine on the mantle. Or maybe you want to hide the label on the cheap wine you're giving as a gift. Perhaps you're like me, and there are just too many wine bottles for the tiny wine rack. This pattern is for you. Not only will it keep your wine in the dark, it'll make it decorative, too. Form and function. Make a few in different colors and proudly flaunt your wine collection and knitting prowess. Plus, this sweater is really just a top-down raglan with a crazily long neck and body. So if you're at all nervous about knitting a sweater, start here.

SIZES
To fit 750ml wine bottle

FINISHED MEASUREMENTS
10½" (27cm) circumference

YARN
1 skein Neighborhood Fiber Co. Studio Sport (wool, 127 yds [116m] per 57g skein)

▶▶▶ *color* ADAMS MORGAN (pictured far left)
▶▶▶ *color* SHERIDAN CIRCLE (pictured near left)

NEEDLES
1 set of 5 size US 3 (3.25mm) DPNs

NOTIONS
buttons (optional)
waste yarn for holders
stitch markers
yarn needle

GAUGE
20 sts and 28 rows = 4" (10cm) in St st

YOKE

CO 24 sts. Pm and join, being careful not to twist. Work even in k2, p2 ribbing for 5" (13cm) for a turtleneck or 2" (5cm) for a mock turtleneck.

RAGLAN SHAPING

Distribute sts on needles as foll:

Needles 1 and 3: 8 sts for front and back.

Needles 2 and 4: 4 sts for sleeves.

Next (Inc) Rnd: *KFB, knit to last 2 sts on needle, KFB, k1; rep from * across each needle.

Rep inc Rnd 8 times more. St count should be as foll:

Needles 1 and 3: 26 sts.

Needles 2 and 4: 22 sts.

DIVIDE BODY AND SLEEVES

Next Rnd: Knit across needle 1. Place sts from needle 2 on waste yarn. Cont knitting across needle 3. Place sts from needle 4 on waste yarn—52 body sts.

Distribute body sts evenly on needles and join in a rnd.

BODY

Work even in St st for 7" (18cm). Work in k2, p2 ribbing for 1" (3cm). BO loosely.

SLEEVES (MAKE 2)

Place 22 sleeve sts on needles, distribute evenly and join in a rnd. Work even in St st for 3½" (9cm). Work in k1, p1 ribbing for ½" (1cm).

BO loosely.

FINISHING

Now you have to close up the little hole in the "armpit." Use mattress st and the tail yarn from the sleeves to seam it closed.

Weave in all ends and block by putting it on a wine bottle to dry.

Wine Cozy

For a more practical vino accessory, make a wine bottle carrier in your favorite colors. This one (pictured at right) is made using Cascade 220 yarn in colors inspired by Harry Potter's Gryffindor House (1 each of colors 2401 maroon and 9476 maize). Using the same yarn held doubled, cast on 40 sts onto size US 15 DPNs. Work in the rnd for 16" (41cm) and then dec sts evenly on every rnd beg with k8, k2tog.

End with 4 sts and pull yarn through rem sts to close the hole. Using the same needles and yarn, knit 32" (81cm) of I-cord. Felt it all and then, using sharp scissors, poke 4 holes in the bag to match the picture. Feed the felted I-cord through the holes to make a little strap. Or, you could sew leather straps onto the bag in place of the I-cord. The possibilities are endless!

Dishrag Trio

By Karida Collins & Libby Bruce

There are a few wonderful things about dishrags. They're meant to wipe up spills, and such a humble purpose makes them truly worry-free knitting—mistakes don't matter too much when a project's destiny is to scour a frying pan. They're wonderfully useful, too. (Spilled drink? No worries. I'll wipe it up with my knitting.) Kitchen cotton is cheap and comes in a staggering array of colors. Plus, there is just something really cool about handmaking something as humble and functional as a dishrag. I'm not saying it will make doing the dishes fun or anything, but seeing your happy little dishrag in the sink will at least brighten your day a bit.

FINISHED MEASUREMENTS

Woozy: 7" (18cm) square
Zigzag: 9" (10½" × 15") (23cm [27cm × 38]cm) square
Ridges Not Rigid: 8" (13") (20cm [33cm]) square

YARN

1 skein Lion Brand Lion Cotton (cotton, 236 yds [216m] per 140g skein) in desired color(s) makes 1 washrag. Use partial skeins to make multicolored rags.

Note: This is a great project for using up leftover bits of yarn!

NEEDLES

size US 7 (4.5mm) straight needles

NOTIONS

yarn needle

GAUGE

16 sts and 24 rows = 4" (10cm) in St st

These dishrags are dedicated to Ann Shayne and Kay Gardiner, for bringing the washrag out of the drawer.

KFB (knit 1 front and back): Inc 1 st by knitting into the front and back of the next st.

K2tog (knit 2 together): Dec 1 st by knitting 2 sts tog.

K3tog (knit 3 together): Dec 2 sts by knitting 3 sts tog.

▶ WOOZY WASHRAG

Diagonal garter stitch is a simple thing, but it feels a little magical when you first learn it. It's done by increasing one stitch on each end of every other row up to the desired width, then decreasing in the same manner. What could be easier?

CO 1 st.

Row 1 (RS): Knit into the front, back and front of st—3 sts.

Next and all WS Rows: Knit.

Next Row: KFB, knit to last st, KFB—5 sts.

Rep last 2 rows, changing colors as desired, until there are 41 sts, ending with a WS row.

Next Row (RS): K2tog, knit to last 2 sts, k2tog—39 sts.

Next and all WS Rows: Knit.

Rep last 2 rows, changing colors as desired, until 3 sts rem. K3tog. Fasten off.

FINISHING

Weave in ends.

ZIGZAG RAG

This stitch pattern from Barbara Walker's *Treasury of Knitting Patterns* combines knit and purl rows to make a really fun final look. Plus the alternate stitch patterns help get the scuzziness off the dishes.

CO 36 (42) sts.

Row 1 and all WS Rows: Purl.

Row 2 (RS): *K3, p3; rep from * to end of row.

Row 4: P1, *k3, p3; rep from * to last 5 sts, k3, p2.

Row 6: P2, *k3, p3; rep from * to last 4 sts, k3, p1.

Row 8: *P3, k3; rep from * to end of row.

Row 10: P2, *k3, p3; rep from * to last 4 sts, k3, p1.

Row 12: P1, *k3, p3; rep from * to last 5 sts, k3, p2.

Rep Rows 1–12 until piece measures 9 (15)" (23 [38]cm). BO.

FINISHING

Weave in ends.

► RIDGES NOT RIGID WASHRAG

Another Barbara Walker stitch pattern, this one is just a variation of knit and purl ridges combined. The idea is that if you alternate Stockinette, reverse Stockinette and garter, the possibilities are endless! Just knit some and purl some. You can't go wrong.

QUAKER RIDGING

Rows 1, 3 & 5: Knit.

Rows 2 & 4: Purl.

Rows 6 & 7: Knit.

Rows 8 & 10: Purl.

Rows 9 & 11: Knit.

Row 12: Knit.

Row 13: Purl.

Row 14: Knit.

Rep Rows 1–14 for patt.

ALL FOOLS' WELT

Row 1: Knit.

Row 2: Purl.

Rows 3–8: Knit.

Rep Rows 1–8 for patt.

CO 32 (52) sts. Work in desired st patt, changing colors as desired, until piece measures 8 (13)" (20 [33]cm). BO.

FINISHING

Weave in ends.

Snakebite Hats

By Libby Bruce

My friend Juan is a zoologist and a knitter, and he is always coming up with design ideas inspired by the animal kingdom. When he suggested that I design a hat with a scarf attached that looked like a snake, I responded, "Try and stop me!"

Knitted from mouth to tail, this whimsical scarf-hat combo is the perfect union of form and function. The beautiful baby alpaca yarn is fantastic to knit with. Since the whole project is knitted in the round, the tail makes an extra warm scarf. Shown here in both garden snake and coral snake colorways, *Snakebite* will keep you cozy all winter long.

FINISHED MEASUREMENTS

Hat circumference: 20" (51cm)

Length: 60" (152cm)

YARN

GARDEN SNAKE

1 skein Cascade Baby Alpaca Chunky (100% baby alpaca, 108 yds [99m] per 100g skein) in each of the foll colors:

▶▶▶ *color* #572 RED (A)

▶▶▶ *color* #561 YELLOW (C)

2 skeins Cascade Baby Alpaca Chunky

▶▶▶ *color* #558 GREEN (B)

CORAL SNAKE

2 skeins Cascade Baby Alpaca Chunky in each of the foll colors:

▶▶▶ *color* #572 RED (A)

▶▶▶ *color* #561 YELLOW (C)

▶▶▶ *color* #561 BLACK (D)

NEEDLES

16" (41cm) size US 10 (6mm) circular needle

1 set of 5 US 9 (5.5mm) DPNs

NOTIONS

2 ¾" (2cm) sew-on wiggle eyes

stitch markers

yarn needle

GAUGE

14 sts and 20 rows = 4" (10cm) in St st

③

K2tog (knit 2 together): Dec 1 st by knitting 2 sts tog.

Pm (place marker): Slip a premade marker or a loosely knotted piece of scrap yarn in a contrasting color onto the right needle after the st just knit to mark a spot in the knitting to refer to on future rows. When you come to a marker, simply slip it from the right-hand needle to the left-hand needle.

BRIM

With circular needle and A, CO 69 sts. Pm and join for working in the rnd, being careful not to twist sts.

Work in k1, p2 rib for 1" (3cm).

Change to St st and foll stripe patt for either the Coral Snake or Garden Snake as foll:

► CORAL SNAKE

Rnds 1–4: Knit with color D.

Rnds 5–8: Knit with color C.

Rnds 9–16: Knit with color A.

Rnds 17–20: Knit with color C.

Rep Rnds 1–20 for the rest of the hat.

► GARDEN SNAKE

Rnds 1–10: Knit with color B.

Rnds 11–15: Knit with color C.

Rep Rnds 1–15 for the rest of the hat.

Work even in patt until piece measures 6" (15cm) from beg.

CROWN DECREASES

Cont as est, dec for crown:

Rnd 1: *K5, k2tog; rep from * to last 6 sts, k6—60 sts.

Rnd 2: Knit.

Rnd 3: *K4, k2tog; rep from * around—50 sts.

Rnd 4: Knit.

Rnd 5: *K3, k2tog; rep from * around—40 sts.

Work even in patt until piece measures 50" (127cm) from beg.

TAIL

Cont as est, dec for tail:

Set-Up Rnd: K20, pm, k20.

Rnd 1: *Knit to 2 sts before marker, k2tog; rep from * around—2 sts dec.

Rnds 2–3: Knit.

Rep Rnds 1–3 until 6 sts rem.

Break yarn. Thread tail through rem 6 sts, fasten off.

FINISHING

Weave in ends. Sew on eyes approx 1" (3cm) above ribbed band.

Six-Pack Carrier

By Libby Bruce

I hate six-packs. They just seem so flimsy, and they're so often wet. I am always afraid the bottom is going to fall out, followed by a cascade of shattering beer bottles. This has never happened to me or to anyone I know, so I think my fears might be a little bit irrational. Still, wouldn't you feel more secure knowing your six-pack was safe, snug and insulated in a custom felted carrier? This simple, fun, quick knit is a great way to keep your bottles safe and cozy.

FINISHED MEASUREMENTS
9" wide × 6" high × 6" deep (23cm × 15cm × 15cm), excluding handles

YARN
1 skein Cascade Pastaza (llama/wool blend, 132 yds [121m] per 100g skein)
▶▶▶ *color #268 YELLOW (A)*
2 skeins Cascade Pastaza
▶▶▶ *color #046 BROWN (B)*

NEEDLES
size US 13 (9mm) straight needles
smaller spare needle

NOTIONS
yarn needle

GAUGE
11 sts and 16 rows = 4" (10cm) in garter st with yarn held double

Note: Yarn is held doubled throughout.

STRIPE PATTERN

Rows 1–4: Knit with color A.

Rows 5–8: Knit with color B.

Rep Rows 1–8.

FRONT AND BACK (MAKE 2)

With 2 strands of A held tog, CO 16 sts. Work even in stripe patt for 9" (23cm), ending with Row 8. BO.

SIDES (MAKE 2)

With 2 strands of A held tog, CO 16 sts. Work even in stripe patt for 6" (15cm), ending with Row 8. BO.

BOTTOM

With 2 strands of B held tog, pick up and knit 20 sts along long edge of front panel. Knit for 6" (15cm). Do not BO. Break yarn.

Using smaller spare needle and B, pick up and knit 20 sts along long edge of back panel.

Connect the back panel with the bottom using a 3-needle BO as foll:

Hold the 2 needles tog with WS facing. Using a third needle, knit the first st of the front needle tog with the first st on the back needle.

Cont to work sts from front and back tog, BO across row.

FINISHING

ASSEMBLE BAG

Whipstitch sides to front and back, aligning so stripe patt is unbroken. Whipstitch sides to bottom.

HANDLES

With 2 strands of B held tog, pick up and knit 18 sts along top edge of front of bag. Knit every row until piece measures 5" (13cm) from pick-up row, ending with a WS row.

Next Row (RS): K5, BO 8, k5.

Next Row: K5, CO 8 over bound-off sts, k5.

Knit 3 more rows, BO.

Rep along top edge of back for opposite handle.

Weave in ends.

Lightly felt to desired size.

Note: Dimensions of six-packs can sometimes vary, so have a sixer of your favorite handy. You know… to measure.

118

Don't Cry Over Spilled Beer

From Karida...

So, maybe you skipped the recommended stain-free drinks (see page 69). And maybe you're also a klutz. Or maybe some drunk jerk just sloshed Guinness all over the beige sweater you're knitting. Don't worry. I know all about spills, stains and how to clean up. Just follow these steps and your stains will come right out.

1. *Absorb*. If you've got wine pooling all over your knitting, first use a clean towel or napkin to absorb the excess liquid. Be careful not to rub the fabric. Rubbing just sets the stain.

2. *Assess the Damage*. How bad is it? If you're in a darkened corner, you can't always see where all the deadly droplets of wine splattered. Get up and head to the bathroom. No matter how dark a bar is, the bathroom is usually well-lit. Or pull out your tiny flashlight. You have one in your notions bag, right?

3. *Triage with Club Soda*. There is a reason this drink is so often recommended for stain removal. It works! If you're in a bar, it should be readily available. Using a clean towel or napkin, dab the club soda on the stain and blot it gently.

This should be enough to handle your immediate stain removal needs. When you get home, use a wool-wash to clean the WIP. I like Soak because it doesn't need rinsing and has even lifted stains from thrift store sweaters. Follow the directions on the bottle. If the yarn is non-superwash, be careful not to scrub the WIP or agitate the water. You don't want to accidentally felt your WIP! Your project may need multiple treatments, but keep at it. You'll have a clean (and exceptionally fragrant) WIP in no time.

Cherry Cordial Cardi

By Libby Bruce

This little shrug was born last winter, when I saw a dress in a catalog and had a vision of myself attending holiday parties in it, along with coordinating cherry red stockings, these black shoes I'd been eyeing, and a warm, stylish little red shrug, which I would make from scratch. I ordered the dress, but it didn't fit. (It is still hanging in my closet, waiting for me to grow the bosoms to fill its cavernous bodice.) The shoes were too expensive. And of course, I never got around to casting on for my shrug. (For the record, the stockings worked out fine.)

Luckily, a few months later when I was designing patterns for this book, I remembered the shrug. Knit from the top down on large needles, *Cherry Cordial* is a knitting vacation for the more experienced knitter and a good next step for a beginner ready to try a sweater.

SIZES
Women's XS (S, M, L, XL, XXL)

FINISHED MEASUREMENTS
Bust: 30 (33, 37½, 40, 44, 48)" (76 [84, 95, 102, 112, 122]cm)

Length: 15 (15½, 17½, 18½, 19, 19½)" (38 [39, 44, 47, 48, 50]cm)

Note: The loose gauge of this shrug allows for significant stretch, so it can be worn with up to 2" (5cm) negative ease.

YARN
7 (8, 9, 10, 11, 12) skeins Karabella Margrite Bulky (wool/cashmere blend, 77 yds [70m] per 50g skein)

▶▶▶ *color #07 RED*

NEEDLES
24" (61cm) size US 10½ (6.5mm) circular needle
1 set of 5 size US 10½ (6.5mm) DPNs
24" (61cm) size US 9 (5.5mm) circular needle
1 set of 5 size US 9 (5.5mm) DPNs

NOTIONS
stitch markers
stitch holders or waste yarn
yarn needle
1 ½" (1cm) button

GAUGE
14 sts and 18 rows = 4" (10cm) in St st using larger needles

BODY

With larger circular needles, CO 53 sts. Do not join, work back and forth in rows.

YOKE

Row 1 (RS): K1, pm, k7, pm, k37, pm, k7, pm, k1.

Row 2 (and all WS Rows): Purl.

Row 3: KFB, sl marker, KFB, k5, KFB, sl marker, KFB, k35, KFB, sl marker, KFB, k5, KFB, sl marker, KFB—61 sts.

Row 4: Purl.

Row 5: KFB, *knit to 1 st before marker, KFB, sl marker, KFB; rep from * to last st, KFB (10 sts inc).

Rep Rows 4–5 until front panels have 8 sts—91 sts.

Next Row (WS): Purl.

Next Row: *Knit to 1 st before marker, KFB, sl marker, KFB; rep from * to end (8 sts inc).

Rep these 2 rows a total of 10 (12, 16, 18, 20, 22) times—171 (187, 219, 235, 251, 267) sts.

Work 1 WS row.

DIVIDE BODY AND SLEEVES

Next Row (RS): Knit to 1st marker, sl 35 (39, 47, 51, 55, 59) sleeve sts onto holder, remove 2nd marker, CO 3 (3, 3, 3, 6, 9) underarm sts, knit across back sts to 3rd marker, sl 35 (39, 47, 51, 55, 59) sleeve sts onto holder, remove last marker, CO 3 (3, 3, 3, 6, 9) underarm sts, knit to end of row—107 (115, 131, 139, 153, 167) sts.

Work even in St st until piece measures 7½" (19cm) from underarm.

BOTTOM RIBBING

Change to smaller circular needles. Work in k1, p1 ribbing, ending with k1, for 1" (3cm). BO loosely in patt.

SLEEVES

Move sts from holder onto larger DPNs. Pick up and knit 3 (3, 3, 3, 6, 9) sts from underarm, pm and join in a rnd—38 (41, 50, 53, 61, 68) sts.

Work even in St st for 12 rnds.

Next (Dec) Rnd: SSK, knit to marker, k2tog (2 sts dec).

Next 2 Rnds: Knit.

Rep last 3 rnds a total of 4 times—30 (33, 42, 45, 53, 60) sts.

Work even until sleeve measures 9" (23cm) from underarm.

Next Rnd (sizes S, L and XL only): Knit to 2 sts before marker, k2tog—30 (32, 42, 44, 52, 60) sts.

Change to smaller DPNs and work in k1, p1 ribbing for 2" (5cm). BO loosely in patt.

Rep for other sleeve.

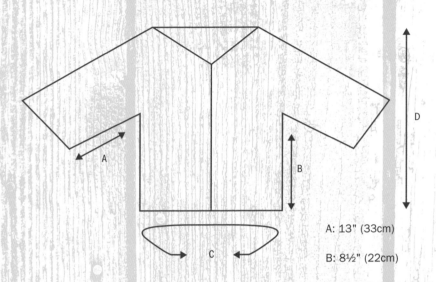

A: 13" (33cm)

B: 8½" (22cm)

C: 30 (33, 37½, 40, 44, 48)" (76 [84, 95, 102, 112, 122]cm)

D: 15 (15½, 17½, 18½, 19, 19½)" (38 [39, 44, 47, 48, 50]cm)

FINISHING

BANDS

With smaller circular needle and RS facing, starting at front right corner, pick up and knit 141 (145, 157, 161, 165, 169) sts up right front edge, around neck and back down left front edge. Work in k1, p1 ribbing, ending with k1, for 3 rows.

Next (Buttonhole) Row (RS): Work in rib for 28 sts, k2tog, yo, cont rib as set to end of row.

Cont in rib for 1 row more. BO in patt.

Weave in ends. Block. Sew button opposite buttonhole.

Zori Coasters

By Karida Collins

Zori are the flat Japanese sandals traditionally worn with kimonos. In the past, zori bases were made with woven rice paper or other plant fibers, and the straps were made with luxurious fabric, often black or red velvet. Now you can get plastic zori in a myriad of colors. But these zoris aren't for your feet at all—they're for your wine glasses (or beer bottles...). Footwear for wine glasses!?! It's not as crazy as it sounds. Make these useful coasters in different colors to distinguish guests' drinks or make a set in one color as a gift to go with a nice bottle of wine. If you like, leave off the "thongs"—the simple stitch pattern for the flat of the sandal makes a lovely and simple square coaster on its own. As a bonus, both yarns used for the sandals are machine washable. If someone spills, just toss them in the washer.

FINISHED MEASUREMENTS
4" (10cm) square

YARN
1 skein Lion Brand Lion Cotton (cotton, 236 yds [216m] per 140g skein)
▶▶▶ *color #112 POPPY RED (A)*
▶▶▶ *color #098 NATURAL (A)*
▶▶▶ *color #136 CLOVE (A)*
1 skein Lion Brand Chenille Thick & Quick (acrylic/rayon blend, 100 yds [91m] (solids) 75 yds [69m] (prints) per skein)
▶▶▶ *color #153 BLACK (B)*
▶▶▶ *color #189 WINE (B)*
▶▶▶ *color #213 RUBY (B)*
Note: Choose one skein for A and one skein for B. One skein of each makes several coasters.

NEEDLES
size US 7 (4.5mm) straight needles
1 set of 2 size US 7 (4.5mm) DPNs

NOTIONS
yarn needle

GAUGE
25 sts and 30 rows = 4" (10cm) in patt st

LINEN STITCH

Row 1: K1, *sl 1 wyif, k1; rep from * to end.

Row 2: K1, p1, *sl 1 wyib, k1; rep from * to last
st, k1.

Rep Rows 1–2.

COASTER

With straight needles and A, CO 25 sts.

Work in linen st until piece measures approx 4"
(10cm). BO.

STRAPS

With DPNs and B, CO 3 sts.

Work in I-cord for approx 10" (25cm). BO.

FINISHING

With yarn needle and A, sew 1 end of the
chenille I-cord to the lower right corner of the
coaster. Sew the other end to the lower left
corner. Pull on the I-cord to form a "V" shape
and sew the point of the "V" down in the center
to create the sandal thong. Depending on the
size of the base of your wine glasses, you might
want to sew down more of the I-cord to make the
thong of the sandal smaller for a snug fit.
Weave in ends. Block lightly if needed.

Tasting Party

From Karida...

As a variation of your Knitter's Night In (see page 45), host a Tasting Party. Yarn Tasting + Wine *and* Chocolate Tasting. You could do wine *or* chocolate, but I'm always up for a little overindulgence.

The idea of the party is that everyone gets to sample little bits of different wines, chocolates and yarns. Ask everyone to bring one bottle of wine for tasting and one ball of a yummy new yarn they want to share. You provide the chocolate. An assortment of truffles is a great idea. Or brownies. Or fudge. Mmmm…chocolate.

Now, you don't have to be a sommelier to host a wine tasting. I've hosted this party with my friend, and we mostly just hang out and taste lots of different wines. Don't let the fact that you don't know the textbook definition of a "dry, oaky" white stop you from having fun!

During the party everyone gets to try the yarns (and wine and chocolate). If you're hosting, it's a good idea to have extra needles around for people to use for swatching. At the end of the night, everyone should have "tasted" lots of gourmet goodies.

A variation of the party is a blind taste test. Without looking at the labels, let guests try to guess the contents of the yarns they're knitting with. Without the label, can you distinguish between qiviut and cashmere? Merino and Blue-Faced Leicester?

K.I.S.S. *Leg Warmers, Cowl & Arm Warmers*

By Karida Collins

One of the most well-known principles of design is abbreviated K.I.S.S. Keep It Simple, Stupid. Form should follow function. If you're going to knit while you're "distracted," this principle should always be your guide. Instead of Keep It Simple Stupid, these accessories encourage you to Keep It Stockinette Stitch. Stockinette stitch in the round is incredibly forgiving, and you'll never be confused about which stitch comes next. These projects celebrate the monotony and encourage you to embrace the Stockinette stitch, curling edges and all. If you're feeling ambitious, you can always add a garter or seed stitch edge to any of these projects to eliminate the curl at the edges.

Leg Warmers

These leg warmers use fun, bulky yarn to make the stitch pattern seem more interesting. Consider making the reverse Stockinette stitch side the outside, and you'll really have some fun with texture!

LEG WARMERS

CO 24 sts. Pm and join, being careful not to twist.

Work in St st until there is just enough yarn left to bind off, approx 13" (33cm) long or desired length. BO.

FINISHING

Weave in ends. Block gently.

FINISHED MEASUREMENTS
12" (30cm) circumference

YARN
2 skeins Neighborhood Fiber Co. Victorian Bulky (wool, 64 yds [59m] per 114g skein)
▶▶▶ *color* BRIGHTWOOD

NEEDLES
1 set of 5 size US 13 (9mm) DPNs

NOTIONS
stitch markers
yarn needle

GAUGE
8 sts and 12 rows = 4" (10cm) in St st

Cowl

The cowl is a great substitute for a scarf. In this case, Stockinette stitch shows off the unique beauty of a hand-painted yarn without competing with the colors. Use Stockinette stitch to experiment with wildly multicolored yarns, and you won't get bored.

COWL

CO 100 sts. Pm and join, being careful not to twist.

Work in St st to 18" (46cm) or desired length.

BO.

FINISHING

Weave in ends. Block gently.

Tip

Remember, you could easily make any of these patterns with different yarns by simply knitting a swatch and multiplying the number of stitches per inch (3 centimeters) by the desired size of your Stockinette stitch tube. These patterns are just the beginning!

FINISHED MEASUREMENTS
20" (51cm) circumference

YARN
2 skeins Neighborhood Fiber Co. Penthouse Spun Silk (silk, 163 yds [149m] per 50g skein)
►►► *color* BROOKLAND

NEEDLES
16" (41cm) size US 7 (4.5mm) circular needle

NOTIONS
stitch markers
yarn needle

GAUGE
20 sts and 24 rows = 4" (10cm) in St st

Arm Warmers

Just because the knitting is all Stockinette stitch doesn't mean you can't have a thumb hole. These arm warmers employ some simple finishing to give the effect of a thumb hole without actually knitting one.

ARM WARMERS

CO 50 sts. Pm and join, being careful not to twist. Work in St st to 10" (25cm) or desired length. BO.

FINISHING

Lay arm warmer flat. Measure 1" (3cm) from side, sew a seam 2" (5cm) down from this point to create thumb opening. Rep on other arm warmer. Weave in ends. Block gently.

FINISHED MEASUREMENTS
8" (20cm) circumference

YARN
2 skeins Neighborhood Fiber Co. Studio Sport (wool, 127 yds [116m] per 57g skein)
►►► *color* GRANT CIRCLE

NEEDLES
1 set of 5 size US 5 (3.75mm) DPNs

NOTIONS
stitch markers
yarn needle

GAUGE
24 sts and 32 rows = 4" (10cm) in St st

Wine Charms

By Karida Collins

In a group of people all drinking wine, sometimes it's hard to remember which glass belongs to which person. Wine charms are the easiest solution to this problem. Just slip them on each guest's glass, and everyone knows which glass is hers. Often, these types of charms are beaded, but what about the knitters? These knitted charms start with a tiny I-cord and make a perfect, fast gift.

FINISHED MEASUREMENTS
1" (3cm) diameter

YARN
small amounts of Neighborhood Fiber Co. Studio Sock (merino wool, 435 yds [398m] per 113g skein) in assorted colors

NEEDLES
1 set of 2 size US 0 (2mm) DPNs

NOTIONS
1" (3cm) metal hoops (as used for beading)
needle-nose or jewelry pliers

GAUGE
Gauge is not important for this project

WINE CHARMS
CO 3 sts.
Work I-cord for 2½" (6cm). BO.

FINISHING
Weave in ends. Carefully slide the straight end of the metal hoop through 1 end of the I-cord tube. Gently feed the rest of the hoop through the tube until only the loop at the end is exposed. Feed the straight end of the hoop through the loop. Using pliers, "close" the hoop by bending the straight end up.

Knitting I-Cord
Use two double-pointed needles to work I-cord. Cast on three stitches onto the first needle. Bring the working yarn behind the stitches to the first stitch on the needle and knit all three stitches. Do not turn. Slide the stitches to the opposite end of the needle. Knit the stitches again. Continue in this manner until the cord reaches the desired length.

Knitters Gone Wild

If you're going to knit with a beer in front of you, you've got to embrace an anything-can-happen attitude. One great way to cultivate this is by making a group project at the bar.

Have all your knitters bring whatever yarn they've got lying around. When you get to the bar, cast on a few stitches and start passing the project around, allowing each knitter to switch the yarn, change the stitch pattern, increase, decrease, change needle size, join in the round…whatever. You could bind off that same night, or keep going at your next knitting happy hour.

Let the project just evolve. At the end you may have something functional, like a crazy scarf to give your favorite bartender, a piece of knitted graffiti, a cozy for the bar stool or an awesome wall hanging. On the other hand, you might have, for example, a giant mitten—completely useless, except for the fact that it is totally fun and reminds you of what it means to go crazy with your needles and your friends. Either way, you win.

Hangover Lap Blanket

By Libby Bruce

We all have the occasional rough morning, especially those of us who love the nightlife. When this happens, the *Hangover Lap Blanket* is your best friend. Knit in the softest baby alpaca yarn, this little lap blanket is ideal for cozying up on the couch and recuperating.

The blanket is knit from the bottom up, with flaps on the top and bottom to hide the color stranding. A decorative garter stitch border on the edges helps the blanket lay flat. The Fair Isle borders—moonshine jugs and first-aid crosses—are bound to put you in a better mood. (They make me giggle every time I see them.)

FINISHED MEASUREMENTS
25" × 35" (64cm × 89cm)

YARN
4 skeins Cascade Baby Alpaca Chunky (baby alpaca, 108 yds [99m] per 100g skein)
► ► ► *color* #565 WHITE (A)
1 skein each of Cascade Baby Alpaca Chunky in each of the foll colors:
► ► ► *color* #572 RED (B)
► ► ► *color* #556 BROWN (C)
► ► ► *color* #553 BLACK (D)

NEEDLES
40" (102cm) size US 10 (6mm) circular needle

NOTIONS
stitch markers
yarn needle

GAUGE
14 sts and 18 rows = 4" (10cm) in St st

Note: This blanket is worked from the bottom up, with a garter st border at the sides and simple stranded colorwork along the top and bottom borders.

BOTTOM HEM

With A, CO 124 sts. Work 12 rows St st, ending with a RS row.

Next Row (WS): Knit to create turning ridge for hem.

BOTTOM BORDER

Next Row (RS): K10, pm, k104, pm, k10.

Next Row (WS): Knit to marker, sl marker, purl to marker, sl marker, knit to end.

Next Row (RS): K10, sl marker, with A and B, work Row 1 of Chart A over 13 sts 8 times across row, sl marker, k10.

Cont to work border sts in garter st and center sts in St st, finish working Rows 2–9 of cross chart.

Work 2 rows as est with A.

Next Row (WS): Knit.

BODY

With A, work as foll:

All RS Rows: Knit.

All WS Rows: Knit to marker, sl marker, purl to marker, sl marker, knit to end.

Work even until piece measures 25" (64cm) or desired length from beg, ending with a RS row.

TOP BORDER

Next Row (WS): Knit.

Work 2 rows as est.

Next Row (RS): Work Chart B over 13 sts 8 times across row using A and C.

Cont to work border sts in garter st and center sts in St st, finish working Rows 2–9 of jug chart.

With A, work 2 rows in St st.

TOP HEM

Next Row (WS): Knit to create turning ridge for hem.

Work 12 rows St st. BO.

FINISHING

With yarn needle and D, embroider XXX symbol on each jug. These don't need to be precise (you've got a hangover, after all).

With WS facing, fold top hem down over stranding. Whipstitch loosely to the back of the blanket. Rep for bottom hem.

Weave in ends. Steam block if desired.

Cross Chart

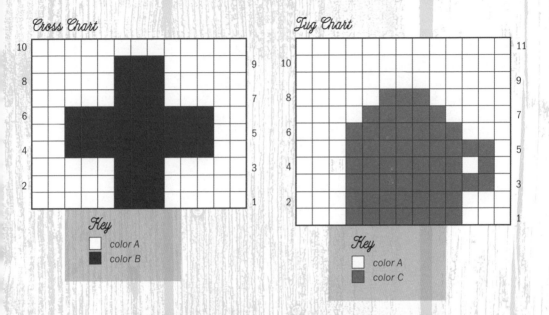

Key
- color A
- color B

Tug Chart

Key
- color A
- color C

Whiskey Sour Messenger Bag

By Ellie Heath

This is a great pattern for the first-time felter or even a beginning knitter. It involves some basic increasing and decreasing, but mostly it is just straight back-and-forth knitting. The great thing about felting is that your stitches don't have to be perfect. After the item is felted, all the stitches blend together to become a sturdy fabric.

I used Cascade Jewel Hand Dyed and doubled the yarn. Jewel comes in an extensive array of beautiful colors and is very affordable for the amount of yarn you get on each skein.

FINISHED MEASUREMENTS
13" high × 17" long × 3½" deep (33cm × 43cm × 9cm), before felting
11" high × 16" long × 3" deep (28cm × 41cm × 8cm), after felting

YARN
8 skeins Cascade Jewel Hand Dyed (wool, 142 yds [130m] per 100g skein)
►►► color #9889 RUST (A)
2 skeins Cascade Jewel Hand Dyed
►►► color #9971 ORANGE (B)

NEEDLES
24" (61cm) size US 15 (10mm) circular needle

NOTIONS
yarn needle

GAUGE
11 sts and 14 rows = 4" (10cm) in garter st before felting

NOTES

KFB (knit 1 front and back): Inc 1 st by knitting into the front and back of the next st.

K2tog (knit 2 together): Dec 1 st by knitting 2 sts tog.

BAG BODY

With A, CO 38 sts. Do not join, work back and forth in rows. Change to B. Knit 4 rows in garter st. Change to A.

***Next (Inc) Row:** KFB, knit to last st, KFB—40 sts.

Knit 4 rows.

Rep from * until there are 46 sts.

Work even in garter st for 32" (81cm) more. BO.

STRAP

With B, CO 10 sts. Work in garter st for 50 rows.

Next (Inc) Row: KFB, knit to last st, KFB—12 sts.

Knit 3 rows.

Next Row: Rep Inc Row—14 sts.

Knit for 24 rows.

Next (Dec) Row: K2tog, knit to last 2 sts, k2tog—12 sts.

Knit for 3 rows.

Next Row: Rep Dec Row—10 sts.

Knit for 50 rows. BO.

FINISHING

Fold the edge of the bag (opposite striped side) up 13" (33cm) for the front of the bag. Place the ends of the strap at the sides of the bag and whipstitch it in place to the front and back, leaving the center portion of strap open for carrying. Weave in the ends.

Place the bag in the washer with a few old pairs of jeans and/or a clean canvas shoe to aid the agitation process. Add ½ cup detergent and run it through the hottest cycle.

After the cycle, check on the bag to see if it has felted down to the desired size. If not, run the bag through another complete cycle. Once the bag has reached its desired size, shape the bag and let it dry flat. If you like, place a small rectangular box inside the bag to help shape it as it dries. The drying process may take up to 24 hours. See Get Felt Up, page 86, for more information on felting.

Tip

To begin, I wound all my yarn on a ball winder. This process makes it easy to double your yarn when knitting as you are able to pull a strand from the middle and outside of the skein without the yarn getting all tangled up.

Knitting Resources

STANDARD KNITTING ABBREVIATIONS

BEG	beginning	P2TOG	purl 2 together
CC	contrast color	P3TOG	purl 3 together
CN	cable needle	PSSO	pass slipped stitch over
DEC	decrease	REM	remaining
DPN(s)	double-pointed needle(s)	RLI	right lifted increase
EST	continue in patt as established	RS	right side
		RT	right twist
FOLL	following	REP	repeat
INC	increase	SKP	slip 1, knit 1, pass slipped stitch over
K	knit	SK2P	slip 1, knit 2 together, pass slipped stitch over
KFB	knit 1 front and back		
K2TOG	knit 2 together	SL	slip
K3TOG	knit 3 together	SSK	slip, slip, knit
LLI	left lifted increase	ST(s)	stitch(es)
LT	left twist	WORK 2 TOG	work 2 together
M1	make one	WS	wrong side
MC	main color	W&T	wrap and turn
P	purl	WYIB	with yarn in back
(IN) PATT	(in) pattern	WYIF	with yarn in front
PM	place marker	YO	yarn over

KNITTING NEEDLE CONVERSIONS

Diameter	US Size	Suggested Yarn Weight
2mm	0	Lace Weight
2.25mm	1	Lace and Fingering Weight
2.75mm	2	Lace and Fingering Weight
3.25mm	3	Fingering and Sport Weight
3.5mm	4	Fingering and Sport Weight
3.75mm	5	DK and Sport Weight
4mm	6	DK, Sport and Aran/Worsted Weight
4.5mm	7	Aran/Worsted
5mm	8	Aran/Worsted and Heavy Worsted
5.5mm	9	Aran/Worsted, Heavy Worsted and Chunky/Bulky
6mm	10	Chunky/Bulky
6.5mm	10½	Chunky/Bulky and Super Bulky
8mm	11	Chunky/Bulky and Super Bulky
9mm	13	Super Bulky
10mm	15	Super Bulky
12.75mm	17	Super Bulky
15mm	19	Super Bulky
20mm	36	Super Bulky

YARN WEIGHT GUIDELINES

Since the names given to different weights of yarn can vary widely depending on the country of origin or the yarn manufacturer's preference, the Craft Yarn Council of America has put together a standard yarn weight system to impose a bit of order on the sometimes unruly yarn labels. Look for a picture of a skein of yarn with a number 1–6 on most kinds of yarn to figure out its "official" weight. Gauge is given over Stockinette stitch. The information in the chart below is taken from www.yarnstandards.com.

	SUPER BULKY [6]	BULKY [5]	MEDIUM [4]
TYPE	bulky, roving	chunky, craft, rug	worsted, afghan, aran
KNIT GAUGE RANGE	6–11 sts	12–15 sts	16–20 sts
RECOMMENDED NEEDLE IN U.S. SIZE RANGE	11 and larger	9 to 11	7 to 9

	LIGHT [3]	FINE [2]	SUPERFINE [1]	LACE [0]
TYPE	dk, light, worsted	sport, baby	sock, fingering, baby	fingering, 10-count crochet thread
KNIT GAUGE RANGE	21–24 sts	23–26 sts	27–32 sts	33–40 sts
RECOMMENDED NEEDLE IN U.S. SIZE RANGE	5 to 7	3 to 5	1 to 3	000 to 1

SUBSTITUTING YARNS

If you substitute yarn, be sure to select a yarn of the same weight as the yarn recommended for the project. Even after checking that the recommended gauge on the yarn you plan to substitute is the same as for the yarn listed in the pattern, make sure to knit a swatch to ensure that the yarn and needles you are using will produce the correct gauge.

FINISHING

SEAMING

Seaming can be a bummer, so we tried to avoid it as much as possible when writing this book. However, there are a few spots where it's unavoidable, and once you get the hang of it, it's not too bad. Mattress stitch is one of the simplest methods of seaming, and it works well for most of the seams in this book. We've included instructions for some seaming methods in the Special Techniques Glossary beginning on page 150.

WEAVING IN ENDS

When you've finished knitting, use a crochet hook or a darning needle to weave in your ends. A darning needle is faster, but a crochet hook is a lifesaver if you've left too short an end. Weave the yarn in securely and then cut off the remaining end close to the fabric. Give it a little stretch and the end will disappear into the knitting.

BLOCKING

Blocking is often optional, and plenty of knitters don't bother with it. It's easy, though, and it can make your knitting look much better. If you have uneven stitches or gaps in your Fair Isle or crumpled lace, blocking can save the day. In the end, though, it's up to you.

If you want to block your knitting, just lay the piece flat on some towels and pin it into the desired size and shape (be careful not to stretch it out too much). Then squirt it with water until it is pretty damp. You can either let it dry like this, or place a thin towel over it and give it a light steam with an iron. Don't move the piece until it is completely dry.

CARING FOR YOUR HANDKNITS

CLEANING

Always check the yarn label for washing instructions. Generally speaking, you should wash your handknits in cold water with a quality wool wash (Soak is a great one). If your yarn is machine washable, use the gentle cycle. Some yarns do fine in the dryer, but most of the time the dryer is off limits. If you're not sure how a yarn will fare in the washing machine or dryer, knit a swatch and run it through the machine first.

To dry a handknit, lay the wet piece flat on a towel and roll it up in the towel a few times to get out the excess water. (Don't wring your handknits or they'll get all stretched out of shape!) Then lay the piece flat to dry.

STORING

Store your handknits folded up in a clean, dry place, such as a dresser or chest. Don't hang your sweaters on a hanger because they'll pull out of shape. I store mine with cedar chips to repel moths and other wool-munching insects, but plenty of people don't trust the natural methods and use mothballs instead. Be careful with these, though, because they're extremely toxic and are especially dangerous to pets and children.

Special Techniques
Glossary

BINDING OFF

Binding off refers to securing stitches, generally at the edge of a garment. The most basic method of binding off is to knit two stitches, then slip the first knit stitch over the second and off the needle. This process is repeated until all the stitches are bound off, or secured. In addition to this method, there are many other ways of binding off. Follow the method specified in the pattern for the best result.

THREE-NEEDLE BIND OFF

A three-needle bind off works well for joining live stitches. This bind off is generally used when two pieces of knitting with the same number of stitches need to be seamed together, such as shoulder seams or the toes of socks. The "live" stitches for both pieces are kept on separate needles and lined up exactly, stitch for stitch. The third needle is used to work the bind off, by inserting it through the first pair of stitches together, knitting them together, knitting the second pair of stitches together and then sliding the first knit stitch over the second and off the needle. Just as for the traditional bind off, this process is repeated until all the stitches have been bound off.

TUBULAR BIND OFF

The tubular bind off produces a very smooth, elastic edge. To bind off tubularly, leave a very long tail and thread the end onto a yarn needle. Weave the needle in and out of the stitches, following the step-by-step instructions outlined on page 74.

CASTING ON

Casting on refers to creating the number of stitches needed for the first row of any project. There are several methods for casting on. In most cases, you may use the method with which you're most comfortable. However, when a specific cast on is indicated in the pattern, it's best to follow that method since the designer most certainly used it for a good reason.

BACKWARD-LOOP CAST ON

This simple cast-on method is often used to add stitches in the middle of a knitted piece as opposed to casting on stitches for the very beginning of a piece. (For example, you might use this method to cast on stitches for a buttonhole.) To cast on with the backward-loop method, simply use your fingers to make a loop in the working yarn, making sure the yarn crosses the base of the loop on the left. Simply slip this loop onto the needle and pull it snug. Repeat to cast on the number of stitches as indicated.

KNITTING ON

This simple cast on is performed almost the same way as regular knitting. It uses two needles. To cast on by knitting on, make a slip knot and slide it onto the left-hand needle. Slip the right-hand needle into the loop knitwise, and knit the stitch, but do not slip the loop of the left needle. Instead transfer the new stitch from the right needle to the left. Repeat to cast on the number of stitches as indicated.

LONG-TAIL CAST ON

Leaving a long tail (approximately ½" to 1" [1cm to 3cm] for each stitch to be cast on), make a slip knot and slide it onto the right needle so the tail falls in front of the needle and the working yarn falls behind it. Insert your thumb and index finger between the yarn ends so the working yarn is around your index finger and the tail end is around your thumb. Maintain tension on the triangle you created by holding the ends with your other fingers. Turn your palm upward to make a V with the yarn. *Bring the needle in front of the loop on your thumb, grabbing it with the needle. Bring the needle over the strand around your index finger, pulling the resulting stitch through the loop on your thumb. Drop the loop off your thumb, and placing your thumb back into the V configuration, tighten the resulting stitch on the needle. Repeat from * for the number of stitches indicated.

PROVISIONAL CAST ON

A provisional cast on creates a row of live stitches that can be joined to another row of live stitches at a later point to create a seamless join. To cast on provisionally, first crochet a chain with a few more stitches than are to be cast on. Use a single knitting needle to knit a stitch into the back of each loop in the chain (much like picking up stitches). Continue knitting as usual. When instructed by the pattern, "unzip" the provisional crochet chain by untying one end (or cutting the yarn) and freeing each stitch. Slide the stitches onto a free needle.

TUBULAR CAST ON

A tubular cast on creates a nice, smooth edge that works well for garments that need an elastic hem, such as socks. It's similar to a provisional cast on in that the first part of it is worked on waste yarn. See page 72 for step-by-step instructions for tubular cast on.

DECREASES

Practically speaking, decreases reduce the number of stitches on the needles. They can also become integrated into the design when worked symmetrically, row after row, to create darts or visible lines of any other type.

KNIT TWO TOGETHER (k2tog)

This decrease is the simplest of all. To create a right-leaning decrease, slip the right-hand needle through the first two stitches on the left-hand needle from front to back, as for a regular knit stitch. Knit the two stitches as one. To knit three together (k3tog), perform the same operation with three stitches instead of two.

SLIP, SLIP, KNIT (SSK)

This decrease slants to the left. Slip the first stitch as if to knit, slip the second stitch as if to knit, then insert the left needle into the fronts of both stitches and knit them together.

SLIP ONE, KNIT ONE (SKP)

This is another left-slanting decrease. Slip one stitch knitwise, knit the next stitch, then pass the slipped stitch over the knit stitch and off the needle (as when binding off).

SLIP ONE, KNIT TWO TOGETHER, PASS SLIPPED STITCH OVER (SK2P)

This is the double decrease version of slip one, knit one (SKP). To perform this decrease, slip the first stitch knitwise, knit the next two stitches together, then pass the slipped stitch off over the knit stitch (as when binding off).

I-CORD

To make I-cord, cast on a small number of stitches, three or four works best, to one DPN. Knit one row. Slide the stitches to the opposite end of the needle without turning the work. * Pulling the yarn across the back, knit one row. Slide the stitches to the opposite end of the needle, again without turning the work. Repeat from *, creating a tube. When you reach the desired length, break the yarn, pulling it tight through all the stitches. Weave the end of the yarn back through the tube. Sew the end of the I-cord to an earflap or mitten cuff to make a handy tie. Or graft the I-cord to knitted fabric with mattress stitch as a decorative element.

INCREASES

Some increases lean to the right, and others to the left. When increases are spread out evenly over several rows, it doesn't really matter which way they slant. However, increases aligned row after row are quite noticeable and become attractive design elements. Following are some of the most common increases.

KNIT ONE FRONT AND BACK (KFB)

An easy way to increase is to knit one in the front and back of a stitch (KFB). To make this type of increase, simply insert your right-hand needle into the next stitch on the left-hand needle and knit the stitch, keeping the stitch on the left-hand needle instead of sliding it off. Then bring your right-hand needle around to the back, knit into the back loop of the same stitch, and slip both stitches off the needle.

MAKE ONE (M1)

This right-leaning increase is made by inserting the tip of the right needle from front to back into the bar between the next stitch and the stitch just knit. Place this loop onto the left needle and knit into the back of it.

MAKE ONE PURLWISE (M1P)

Increase one stitch by picking up, from back to front, the bar between the next stitch and the stitch just knit and placing it on the left needle. Knit into the front of the picked-up stitch.

LIFTED INCREASES (RLI AND LLI)

When aligned vertically, lifted increases create a defined line that makes it appear as though the increase was made a row below where it was actually created. Right- and left-lifted increases are paired to create strong lines for shaping garments.

Right Lifted Increase (RLI): To create a right-leaning increase, use the right needle to lift the right leg of the stitch below the next stitch to be worked and place it on the left needle. Knit the new stitch.

Left Lifted Increase (LLI): To create a left-leaning increase, use the left needle to lift the left leg below the stitch just knit onto the left needle. Knit the new stitch.

PICKING UP STITCHES

To pick up a stitch, insert the tip of one needle through the side of a stitch from front to back. Leaving about a 3" to 4" (8cm to 10cm) tail, wrap the yarn around the needle as you would for a regular knit stitch. Bring the yarn through the stitch, creating a loop on your needle. This loop is the first picked-up stitch. Continue to pick up the number of stitches required, making sure to space them evenly.

PLACING (AND SLIPPING) A MARKER (PM AND SL MARKER)

Sometimes a pattern calls for you to place a marker (pm) and slip a marker (sl marker). Markers are generally small plastic rings that slide onto a needle and rest in between stitches, marking a certain spot. If you don't have markers on hand, cut small pieces of scrap yarn in a contrasting color. Tie the scrap yarn around the needle in the indicated spot in a loose knot. Move the marker from one needle to the other when you come to it. Continue as usual.

SEAMING

Two main methods are used to seam knitted pieces together in this book. Mattress stitch is used to seam pieces with bound-off edges together, or to seam pieces together along their sides. Kitchener stitch is used to graft two rows of live stitches together. Both methods create a seamless join from the right side, and Kitchener stitch is seamless from both the front and back of the work.

KITCHENER STITCH (KITCHENER ST)

To graft with Kitchener stitch, line up both sets of live stitches on two separate needles with the tips facing the same direction. Thread a yarn needle onto the tail of the back piece. Begin by performing the following steps once: Bring the needle through the first stitch on the needle closest to you as if to purl, leaving the stitch on the needle. Then insert the needle through the first stitch on the back needle as if to knit, leaving the stitch on the needle. Now you are ready to graft. * Bring the needle through the first stitch on the front needle as if to knit, slipping the stitch off the needle. Bring the needle through the next stitch on the front needle as if to purl, leaving the stitch on the needle. Then bring the needle through the first stitch on the back needle as if to purl, sliding the stitch off the needle. Bring the needle through the next stitch on the back needle, leaving the stitch on the needle. Rep from * until all the stitches are grafted together.

Approximately every 2" (5cm), tighten up the stitches, starting at the beginning of the join. Slip the tip of the yarn needle under each leg of each Kitchener stitch and pull up gently until the tension is correct. Repeat across the entire row of grafted stitches. It may help you to say to yourself, "Knit, purl—purl, knit" as you go.

MATTRESS STITCH (MATTRESS ST)

You'll work mattress stitch differently depending on if you are seaming vertically or horizontally. For both vertical-to-vertical and horizontal-to-horizontal seaming, you'll begin the same way. Place the the blocked pieces side-by-side with Right Sides facing. With yarn needle and yarn, insert the needle from back to front through the lowest corner stitch of one piece, then in the lowest corner stitch of the opposite piece, pulling the yarn tight to join the two pieces.

To work vertical-to-vertical mattress stitch, work back and forth as follows: On the first piece, pull the edge stitch away from the second stitch to reveal a horizontal bar. Insert the needle under the bar and pull through. Insert the needle under the parallel bar on the opposite piece and pull through. Continue in this manner, pulling the yarn tight every few rows. Weave the end into the Wrong Side of the fabric.

To work horizontal-to-horizontal mattress stitch, work back and forth as follows: With bound-off stitches lined up stitch-for-stitch, insert the needle under the first stitch inside the bound-off edge to one side and pull it through, then under the parallel stitch on the other side and pull it through. Continue in this manner, pulling the yarn tight every few rows. Weave the end into the Wrong Side of the fabric.

SHORT ROWS

When a pattern includes short rows, you will be working partial rows, knitting or purling only a certain number of stitches before wrapping the yarn and turning the work midway through the row. Short rows create unique effects in knitted fabric, including causing the piece to swirl in a circle or to ripple. To work short rows, you'll need to perform the following two operations.

(RS) Wrap and Turn (W&T): On the Right Side of the work, and with yarn in front, slip one stitch from left needle to right. Move the yarn to the back, slip the stitch back to the left needle, turn work. One stitch has been wrapped.

(WS) Wrap and Turn (W&T): On the Wrong Side of the work, and with yarn in back, slip one stitch from left needle to right. Move the yarn to the front, slip the stitch back to left needle, turn work. One stitch has been wrapped.

Whenever you come to a wrap, work the wrap together with the stitch it wraps. To pick up a wrap and its stitch, slide the tip of the right needle into the wrap from the front of the work and place the wrap on the left needle alongside the stitch it wraps. Knit the two loops together.

Contributors

This book was a blast to write, but we definitely couldn't have done it alone. We were so lucky to have had such talented designers contribute their time and hard work to *Pints & Purls.* Take a minute to get to know these fabulous people, many of whom have their own designs, Web sites and companies you can check out!

Olga Buraya-Kefelian

Olga has been knitting since the age of four, and in recent years she has begun designing her own garments. She currently lives in Virginia with her husband and a crazy cat, where she designs and teaches craft to residents of the greater DC area. You can find her designs in various books and magazines. She enjoys the challenge that each technique can bring and is mesmerized by the world of fashion blended with classics.

You can see more of her adventures in the vast world of craft at *www.olgajazzy.com.*

Kate Chiocchio

Kate is a mad dyer and clinical social worker living in the wilds of suburban Maryland with her family and a whole lot of wool. She spins instead of cleaning the house and knits during soccer games and swim banquets. You can see her yarns and spinning fibers and read about her fiber and family adventures at *dragonflyfiberdesigns.blogspot.com*.

Holly Daymude

Holly Daymude is the retail manager of Knit Happens, an LYS in Alexandria, Virginia. She has been knitting for about five years. She loves knitting socks and always has a few pairs on the needles. Holly's favorite pasttime, other than knitting, is knitting and drinking wine.

Ellie Heath

Ellie Heath hails from the small town of Minocqua, in the beautiful lake country of the Wisconsin Northwoods. After earning a degree in political science from the University of Wisconsin, she moved to Washington, DC, where she worked for one of Wisconsin's U.S. Senators for six years.

A curiosity about knitting turned to passion after a stint working at Stitch DC, along with weekly knitting sessions at the Pharmacy Bar in the DC neighborhood of Adams Morgan.

When she isn't knitting, Ellie lives and works in DC's Capitol Hill neighborhood with her boyfriend and two cats, Stanley and Buddy.

Lindsay Henricks

Lindsay Henricks learned to knit during her first year of college. After going on to get three degrees (none of which are even remotely related to fiber arts, or any art for that matter), she made knitting her career. Now she has her own hand-dyed yarn business and manages a yarn shop. Lindsay's politics, religious studies and secondary education advisors would be so proud. Who knows what she'll do next? She sure doesn't. So check out her blog at *www.thestormmoon.blogspot.com*. Perhaps this time next year she'll be a tree surgeon.

Kathleen Lawton-Trask

Kathleen Lawton-Trask lives in Alexandria, Virginia, with her husband and an anxious tuxedo cat named Gertrude, neither of whom understand the whole strings-and-sticks thing. Kathleen has been knitting for twenty years, but she's still prone to errors. A writer and editor by day, in the evening she reads *Wodehouse*, knits socks and plots knitters' world domination. Come the revolution, she'll spare the cat and maybe the husband. You can find her at *www.knitlikeyoumeanit.com*.

Danielle Romanetti

Danielle Romanetti is the creator of Knit-a-Gogo, which offers knitting classes, unique knitting parties and one-of-a-kind retreats in the Washington, DC, metro area. Danielle is a self-proclaimed environment nut and loves to cook with locally grown and organic foods. She lives in Alexandria, Virginia, with her boyfriend, Phillip, and her two Italian greyhounds, Kirby and Heinz.

Resources

Many of the yarns and supplies used to make the projects in this book can be found in your local yarn store. If you have trouble finding exactly what you want, use the manufacturer information provided here to find online and local vendors.

CASCADE YARN
800.548.1048
http://cascadeyarns.com

ELLA RAE YARNS
Distributed in North America by Knitting Fever, Inc. (K. F. I.)
P.O. Box 336
315 Bayview Avenue
Amityville, NY 11701
516.546.3600
www.knittingfever.com

KARABELLA YARNS INC.
1201 Broadway
New York, NY 10001
800.550.0898
www.karabellayarns.com

LEXIE BARNES
116 Pleasant Street, Studio 245
Easthampton, MA 01027
413.303.1440
http://lexiebarnes.com

LION BRAND YARN
135 Kero Road
Carlstadt, NJ 07072
800.258.YARN (9276)
http://lionbrand.com

C*EYE*BER FIBERS
3500 Boston Street
Suite 431, MS#41
Baltimore, MD 21224
www.ceyeberfiberyarns.com

MISSION FALLS
5333 Casgrain #1204
Montreal, Qc
H2T 1X3
Canada
877.244.1204
http://missionfalls.com

NEIGHBORHOOD FIBER CO.
http://neighborhoodfiberco.com

SHIBUIKNITS, LLC
1101 SW Alder Street
Portland, OR 97205
503.595.5898
http://shibuiknits.com

THE FIBRE COMPANY
Distributed by Kelbourne Woolens
915 N 28th Street, 2nd Floor
Philadelphia, PA 19130
215.687.5534
http://thefibreco.com

Index

A–C

Abbreviations, knitting, 146

Absinthe Sweater, 71–74

Advanced projects. *See* Designated driver projects

Arm warmers, 133

Backward-loop cast on, 150

Bag, messenger, 83–84, 143–144

Barfly Pullover, 59–61

Belt, belly warmer, 33–34

Binding off, 150

Blocking, 149

Cable needle, 27

Caps, 39–40, 43–44. *See also* Hats

Casting on, 150–151

Charts, reading, 21

Cherry Cordial Cardi, 121–123

Circular needles, 93

Cleaning handknits, 149

Coasters, 125–126

College Colors Cozies, 99

Cowl, 131

Cozies, 99, 101–102

Crochet hooks, 27

D–G

Dancing Bamboo Socks, 29–31

Decreases, 151

Dishrag Trio, 109–111

Don't Forget Your Mittens, 79–81

Double-pointed needles (DPNS), 93

Drink ratings, 15

Drink-Like-a-Fish Cozy, 101–102

Drinks, no-stain, 69

Dropped stitches, fixing, 37

Drunken Sweater, 47–49

Entrelac pattern, 17–20

Felting, 84, 86, 101, 143

Finishing, 149

Fizzy Sweater, 67–68

Fox in Socks, 23–25

Group project, 137

H–K

Hangover Lap Blanket, 139–140

Happy Hour Cappy, 39–40

Haramaki Belly Warmer, 33–34

Hats, 91–92, 113–114. *See also* Caps

I-cord, 56, 135, 151

Increases, 152

K.I.S.S. Leg Warmers, 129

Knitting abbreviations, 146

Knitting needle conversions, 147

Knitting needles
cable, 27
circular, 93
DPNS, 93

Knitting on, 150

Knitting-friendly bar, 13

L–O

Leg warmers, 129

Linden Wrap, 17–20

Long-tail cast on, 151

Mistakes, 37, 41

Mitten/scarf combo, 79–81

Movie night, 64

Notions bag, 27

Ol' Pappy Cappy, 43–44

P–R

Picking up stitches, 152

Project ratings
designated driver, 15, 17–25
1 drink, 15, 29–31, 29–34
3 drinks, 15, 39–74 15, 79–126
4 drinks, 15, 129–144

Provisional cast on, 151

Raspberry Wheat Ale Messenger Bag, 83–84

Ruff Neck Warmer, 63–64

S–T

Scarf
horizontal, 89
one-by-one ribbing, 63–64
reversible, with I-cord ties, 55–56

scarf/hat combo, 113–114

scarf/mitten combo, 79–81

Seaming, 149, 152–153

Short rows, 153

Sideways Scarf, 89

Six-Pack Carrier, 117–118

Slouchy Hat, 91–92

Snakebite Hats, 113–114

Social knitting, 11–12

Socks, 23–25, 29–31, 51–52

Stain removal, 119

Stitches
diagonal garter, 110
Kitchener, 152–153
mattress, 153
Stockinette, 47–49, 63–64, 91–92, 129, 131, 133
zigzag, 111

Storing handknits, 149

Sweater
asymmetrical, 47–49
cardi, 121–123
puff rib pattern, 67
pullover, 59–61, 71–74
wine bottle, 105–106

Tank top, 95–96

Tasting party, 127

Three-needle bind off, 150

Tie-One-On Scarf, 55–56

Tubular bind off, 74, 150

Tubular cast on, 72, 151

Two-Fisted Tank, 95–96

U–Z

Waste yarn, 27

Weaving in ends, 149

Weaving Way Socks, 51–52

Whiskey Sour Messenger Bag, 143–144

Wine Bottle Sweater, 105–106

Wine Charms, 135

Wrap, entrelac, 17–20

Yarn swap, 45

Yarn weight guidelines, 148

Yarns, substituting, 148

Zori Coasters, 125–126

Keep Knitting

DOMIKNITRIX
Jennifer Stafford

Whip your knitting into shape. Inside *DomiKNITRix*, you'll find a no-nonsense, comprehensive guide to essential knitting operations and finishing techniques, including step-by-step instructions for all the basic stitches used in the book. Then get your hands dirty with more than 20 spicy projects to satisfy any knitting appetite. Projects range from smaller items like naughty candy heart pillows and a mohawk hat to larger, more complicated pieces like the L'il Red Riding Hoodie and a men's sweater vest with an anatomically correct skull. Just let the DomiKNITrix show you how it's done.

ISBN-13: 978-1-58180-853-7
ISBN-10: 1-58180-853-4
flexibind case, 256 pages, Z0171

GLAM KNITS
Stefanie Japel

Glam Knits showcases 26 totally glam designs by Stefanie Japel, best-selling author of *Fitted Knits*. Each of the *Glam Knits* pieces is knit with decadent luxe yarns that are a pleasure to knit and wear. Whether you choose to knit a sinfully soft cashmere cardigan or an eye-catching metallic dress, you'll be the walking definition of glamour when you wear your finished creation. The *Glam Knits* collection is rounded out with stylish accent pieces like a lacy scarf and even a fluffy fur collar. Every design is easily customizable for a perfect fit, and each pattern is given in sizes from extra small to extra large.

ISBN 13: 978-1-60061-035-6
ISBN 10: 1-60061-035-8
paperback with flaps, 144 pages, Z1378

These books and other fine North Light books are available at your local bookstore or online supplier. Or visit our Web site, *www.mycraftivity.com.*